God Bless You

Though others send you greetings
  now,
  Each couched in phrases fair,
Oh they can be no more sincere
  Than is my simple prayer.

For simple things are worthy
  things:
  Spring breezes that caress you—
The bird that in the twilight
  sings—
  This time-worn phrase:
    "God bless you."

Three simple words each filled
  with love
  In dreary times of stress, you
Will always know I still repeat;
  My simple prayer, "God bless
  you."

Joe Kotcka

173D

DESIGN COPR. 1955 DEVOTIONAL PUBLISHING CO. LITHO IN U.S.A.

KHRUSHCHEV
OF THE UKRAINE

VICTOR ALEXANDROV

KHRUSHCHEV
OF THE UKRAINE

A BIOGRAPHY

PHILOSOPHICAL LIBRARY INC. ● NEW YORK

Translated from the French
by Paul Selver and Wade Baskin

CONTENTS

KHRUSHCHEV
OF THE UKRAINE

EARLY YEARS AT KALINOVKA

Kalinovka, in the southern area of the administrative district of Kursk, is an insignificant little village, and, like hundreds of others of the same kind, it forms part of the Ukraine. A few dozen cottages skirt a small river. Their thatched roofs, discolored by sun and rain, look like dark patches among the bright verdure which dominates the village. On all sides there are cherry trees. Ash trees and weeping willows surround a pond which is now used for washing purposes. Not far away, pigs are wallowing in a quagmire.

A bell tinkles feebly from the tumbledown belfry of the small parish church. Father Amvrossi, the parish priest, is summoning his congregation to prayer. A small boy, with sturdy legs and broad shoulders, is running on ahead of the rest. He takes no notice of the other boys, who are shouting: "Nikita! Nikita! Come fishing with us," but runs faster still towards a cottage on the outskirts of the village. This is the home of Khrushchev the blacksmith.

1

Young Nikita is in a hurry: if he is late his brothers and sisters will have eaten up the dumplings and fruit pasties.

The children take their seats round a huge soup tureen. While they eat, their mother prepares some food for Sergyey Khrushchev, who is working in the forge. To the fruit pasties she adds a large piece of bacon, the favorite dish of the Ukrainians, together with a small bottle of brandy.

Sergyey Khrushchev is a man with a great appetite for food and drink. He is a worthy descendant of the Zaporog Cossacks who were exiled from their Republic by the Russian Tsars. These Cossacks were renowned for their abilities as trenchermen, and also for the amount of liquor which they could stand. Nor did they change their character in this respect when they migrated to the provinces of Kuban and the Ukraine.

Nykola (Nicholas) Khrushch (this word means "chafer" in Ukrainian) settled at Kalinovka in the seventeenth century. The Khrushch clan were famous for their big appetites, their exuberant and unruly temperaments and also for their addiction to the bottle.

By the nineteenth century, when a general census was carried out at the orders of Tsar Nicholas I, the Khrushch clan had added the Russian suffix -ev to their Ukrainian name and thus became Khrushchev. The former Ukrainian Cossacks were now Russified. They spoke Russian with a strong Ukrainian accent and with a phraseology which often sounds quaint to the Russian ear, a phraseology, it may be added, of which even Gogol, the famous Russian author, was never able to rid himself.

When in 1938 Nikita Khrushchev came to Kiev as the general secretary of the Ukrainian communist party, appointed by Stalin, he spoke Ukrainian badly, and it took him two years to learn his "native language." Being an adroit politician, he made up for this shortcoming by energetically espousing the cause of the "Greater Ukraine." Between 1938 and 1940 a large number of books about Khrushchev were published at Kiev, all of them written in a spirit nothing short of devotional.[1]

Nikita's great-grandfather, who was transmuted from "Khrushch" to "Khrushchev" under the auspices of Tsar Nicholas I, was quite a small farmer with his 16 acres of land and a little wood near the River Vorskla (this river crosses the administrative districts of Kursk, Kharkov and Poltava, and flows into the Dniepr near Perevolochna. It was there that Charles XII, after his defeat at Poltava, managed to cross the Dniepr and escape from Prince Menshikov's cavalry). He also had a pasturage of sorts. Sergyey Khrushchev, Nikita's father, had retained nearly all this property, and in his boyhood he looked after two goats, a few pigs and two cows belonging to his father. This is practically all that is known about those activities of his as a "shepherd" which are mentioned in the Kremlin official biographies and the foreign press.

Nikita was a high-spirited lad, fond of sparring with his playmates, angling in the river and setting traps for foxes, whose skins fetched a few kopecks in the village market. With the proceeds he bought a "sopilka," a small Ukrainian flute, on which he used to play for the amusement of his young friends. He was also a champion in a game called "lapta," a species of Russian baseball.

He was not exactly keen on going to school. Father Amvrossi, who, in addition to being the parish priest, taught the village children to read and write, to do sums and, above all, "sacred history" from the Old and New Testaments, rarely saw Nikita in the classroom. That is why Nikita was

[1] One of them, by Nikola Lapko, which appeared in 1939, gives many particulars about Khrushchev's Ukrainian origins, and some of the details about his early years have been utilized in the present volume.

"bezgramotny," that is to say, illiterate, a circumstance with which his official biographers deal delicately by blaming it on to Tsarism.

Sergyey Khrushchev paid very little attention to his land, leaving the duties connected with it to his wife and children, of which he had ten. He had a blacksmith's shop on the high-road leading to Kharkov. There he used to shoe horses, and he had also a small workshop where he repaired locks. When Nikita was eleven years old, his father decided to train him as a locksmith and blacksmith. Nikita himself would have preferred to stay where he was, but Sergyey was a father of the old-fashioned kind who would stand no nonsense. Accordingly the shepherd became a blacksmith-locksmith.

We are told but little about his work in the blacksmith's shop and his leisure activities, his rambles in the woods, his angling, the evening sing-songs on the village green, where Nikita entertained his friends by coaxing Ukrainian folk-tunes from his little flute.

Then he began to grow up. The boy became a youth. He took an interest in girls, and the girls were by no means in-different to his interest.

Soon, with his flute, he was the cock of the walk in the village. Sometimes he sang folk-songs, and he was always the leader when they performed a round dance. He was a very good dancer, and he did the "gopak" particularly well. This dance calls for the ability to make reckless leaps, which he did, with his legs bent and a fierce gusto worthy of the Zapo-rog Cossacks. Then there were the dances of the boys and girls together, and the "boys' dance," in which sticks took the place of the curved swords used by the Cossacks. These sum-mer-time amusements often ended up in a rough and tumble, and the dancers then took advantage of the situation to wipe off old scores.

Nikita handled his stick with remarkable skill. He had

never been taught fencing, but he displayed such adroitness that if this village youth had had to tackle a Polish gentleman, the high-born fencer would have had difficulty in holding his own. It must be added that Nikita, who ruled the roost at Kalinovka, had a number of enemies, and it needed much skill on his part to get through the "boys' dance" without coming to grief.

He was sixteen years of age when he first tasted brandy and also a Ukrainian liqueur called "spotykatch," a name derived from the word "spotikati," which means "to stagger." But it did not make Nikita stagger. Alcohol affected him as little as fatigue when he demonstrated his prowess as a crack dancer.[1]

The place where Sergyey Khrushchev worked now began to look more and more like a real workshop. By this time it was equipped with a second-hand drill, bought at Byelgorod, and a boring-machine bought at Kursk. Other implements were added in due course. Under the supervision of his father Nikita became a skilled turner and fitter. He spent his time repairing agricultural machinery. At this period such machinery was not used to any extent by the small farmers, but landed proprietors in the surrounding areas, for example, Lukyanovitch and Prince Kozlovsky, had brought their custom to the workshop, and the Khrushchev family began to make money.

Young Nikita was a good worker and did not lack leisure for his amusements as before. Reading did not appeal to him, and he was not attracted even by the cheap books which an itinerant hawker used to foist off on the people of Kalinovka. These books were trashy in the extreme, but the youngsters read them eagerly. They failed, however, to arouse Nikita's interest, and he often did not get beyond the second or third

[1] All these details of the early life of Khrushchev are taken from the memoirs of Vladimir Stepanovitch Andriyevsky, a Ukrainian agrarian now residing at Saskatchewan. He is a native of Kalinovka and his book, *The Memoirs of An Agrarian*, is in the Ukrainian language.

page. Vladimir Andriyevsky, who mentions these details, tells us that he found Nikita really absorbed in a book only on one single occasion, the volume in question being Rubakin's popular work on natural history and geology. When he had read it, Nikita expressed his unqualified approval. Evidently the only subject which interested him was science, but the conditions of life in a backward village did not enable him to improve his mind as he otherwise would no doubt have done.

Matters took a new turn when a stomach ulcer prevented his father from working, and Nikita had to take his place. His thick-set figure could often be seen at the anvil, wielding a hammer with might and main. He now worked steadily, and did not often make his appearance on the village green to share in the amusements of the other young people, as in the past. Nikita was beginning to take life seriously. The only relaxation in which he now indulged was fishing. He had bought a small boat, a kind of canoe, and armed with a paddle and some fishing lines he used to make his way downstream towards the marshlands owned by Prince Kozlovsky, which were connected with the river by a large pond. Nikita's boat, which drew very little water, could reach the marshlands by way of the pond. Thereupon he would open a bag which he had hidden in a box, and take out a kind of dragnet which he lowered into the marsh. His catch always consisted of several dozen plump tench which agreeably supplemented the family's ordinary diet. Moreover, fish-food had become a necessity to Sergyey Khrushchev, whose illness was getting worse, and Nikita redoubled his efforts to maintain an ample supply of fish for his father's benefit.

One day he was caught red-handed by the Prince's gamekeeper, who, after knocking him about, tied him hand and foot and delivered him up to the local police sergeant. This dignitary decided to take the law into his own hands. He confiscated the canoe, the fishing lines and dragnet for his own personal benefit, and, after giving Nikita a taste of his "naga-ika," a whip whose lash was weighted with a piece of lead at the end of it, he let him go.

In this way, young Khrushchev, a descendant of the proud Zaporog Cossacks, gained his first experience of social injustice and fell foul of one of the authorities of Imperial Russia. This incident fundamentally affected the subsequent course of his life.

Soon after that, Sergyey Khrushchev died, leaving a large family behind him. It was his widow's wish that Nikita should continue his father's work, while the rest of the family looked after the farm. Since the day when the police sergeant had inflicted corporal punishment on him, Nikita showed himself rarely in the village. Everybody there had heard what had happened to him, and he had a feeling that he was being laughed at. He therefore took to roaming about in the woods by himself, and on these occasions he carried a small book with him, the work of a terrorist named Kravchinsky who was condemned to death during the reign of Alexander II. He escaped from Russia and later settled in England, where he became known as an author under the name of Stepniak. (He was killed by a train at Barnes level crossing.)

"Let us proceed to conquer our country by force of arms. Let us sweep away social injustice. Death to the Tsar's police!" These words formed the keynote of the book. They expressed the basic ideas which inspired the activities of the nihilist revolutionaries who assassinated Alexander II for having, in their opinion, hesitated too long to give land to the peasants and a constitution to Russia.

Young Khrushchev was carried away by the discovery of a world hitherto new to him. In his eyes the police sergeant's "nagaika" typified the horrors of Tsarist Russia which Stepniak-Kravchinsky urged his readers to destroy. The bruises which he still bore on his body were precisely those "stigmas of shame" which, Stepniak-Kravchinsky insisted, must be wiped out by bloodshed.

After this, Nikita decided that he could no longer live in peasant surroundings, the most ignominious aspect of Imperial Russia. He told his mother that he intended to leave home and find employment at Kharkov. The workshop would have to be sold. And in the spring of 1911 he went to Kharkov, the capital of the Ukraine.

II

REVOLUTIONARY BEGINNINGS

At Kharkov, Nikita found employment as turner's mate in the Helferich-Sade factory, which turned out agricultural machinery. His wages amounted to only ten roubles monthly, but on this he managed to live and even to send his mother three roubles a month. He lived with relatives in a suburb of Kharkov known as "Kholodnaya Gora" (Cold Hill), and his room cost him nothing.

These relatives of his worked in the railway-engine repair shops. They belonged to the "younger branch" of the Khrushchev clan, and were the descendants of Nikifor Khrushchev, his great-uncle. Nikifor figures in the revolutionary history of Russia, for he was a member of the nihilists at Kharkov who decided to assassinate the governor general, Prince Kropotkin, the aide de camp of Alexander II and the cousin of Prince Peter Kropotkin, the famous revolutionary who lived for many years in England. Nikifor managed to escape from Si-

9

beria, where he had been condemned to penal servitude, and he then went to America. He died at Pittsburgh.[1]

Nikita now found himself in entirely new surroundings. His cousins were workmen with revolutionary ideas, belonging either to the social democratic or social revolutionary party. The latter were Marxists, while the former were known as "populists." Peter Lavrov, their spokesman, did not recognize the "social determinism" of Marx. He insisted that the individual should discover where the truth lay by criticizing existing conditions, and that he should struggle on behalf of that truth. The Marxists were opposed to individualism in history, whereas the "populists" eagerly welcomed the idea of a "rational and dynamic leader." They also believed that Russia, unlike other countries, would be able to proceed directly from capitalism to socialism. This belief was not shared at that period by the social democrats, the mensheviks and the bolsheviks.

In the house in which Nikita lived at Kharkov there was plenty of literature of the kind known as "illicit," that is to say, prohibited by the Russian authorities because of the political ideas which it promoted. It consisted of socialist books and pamphlets, most of them issued at Rostov-on-the-Don by the firm of Paramonov. These included mainly the works of Marx, Lavrov and Tchernyshevsky, the two latter being exponents of "populism." Tchernyshevsky was not only an important political writer, but also a novelist of distinction, whose *What Is To Be Done?* is a classic work of Russian fiction.

Nikita now became a passionate reader. A new world revealed to him its "truths" and he became aware of a "new social justice." But although he worked hard and read much, he still found time for amusements and rambles. On Sundays

[1] An account of Nikifor Khrushchev is given by the famous Russian author Vladimir Korolenko in his *Memoirs Of My Contemporary*.

he would take his fishing tackle to the outlying district of
Zhuravlevha, where there was a small river called the Nyet-
yetch. Sometimes he ventured as far as the village of Dergat-
chi on the Kharkov-Byelgorod railway route, where there
were fish ponds. In the evening he liked going with his little
cousin Marfa to the popular dancing hall at Pokotilovka. The
toughs who frequented this resort spoke a jargon of their
own, a hodgepodge of Russian, Polish and Yiddish, the latter
element imported from Warsaw and Odessa.

In September 1911 the revolutionary circles at Kharkov
were worked up to a high pitch of excitement. During a performance at the Grand Theatre in Kiev, Stolypin, the President of the Council, had been assassinated by the anarchist
Dimitri Bogrov, who was an agent of the "okhrana" or Tsarist
secret police, and also of the terrorist organization of southern Russia. There was a good deal of mystery about this assassination. Colonel Kulyabko, chief of the secret police at
Kiev, was directly involved in it, and the Tsarina, who made
no secret of her detestation of Stolypin, indirectly. It may be
added that Stolypin was the arch-enemy of Rasputin.

The revolutionaries of Kharkov knew that Bogrov, a Kiev
barrister, had become an agent of the secret police, while still
a member of a terrorist organization, for the express purpose
of gaining admittance to the theatre and assassinating Stolypin there. Stolypin, the most dangerous enemy of the extremists, had just urged that the communal land should be divided
up among the peasants. His object was to destroy the "mir"
or rural commune, without which, according to Lavrov and
Tchernyshevsky, the peasantry would be unable to pass directly from "feudal capitalism" to "integral socialism."

A meeting was held outside the city, near the village of
Sokolniki, "as a mark of respect to Bogrov and in memory of
this martyr of Tsarism" (Bogrov was hanged in the prison of
Lukyanovka at Kiev). This meeting played a very important

part in Nikita's life. He went there with his four cousins to manifest his solidarity with a crowd of some 3,000 people. It had been camouflaged as a popular festivity, and the crowd had brought sandwiches, fruit and vodka with them to emphasize this impression.

Several speakers addressed the meeting, Nikita among them. Thus, when scarcely eighteen years of age he made his first public appearance as a revolutionary. In a book by Makar Ptitza, which was published at Kiev in 1940, the meeting is described as follows:

. . . Comrade Khrushchev was the last speaker. He was still very young, scarcely twenty (this is incorrect; he was not yet eighteen). He was introduced as "the young comrade from the Helferich-Sade factory," and with considerable feeling he uttered a few sentences. He ended his remarks by saying: "Other strugglers will take Bogrov's place."

Even Ptitza, who writes as a humble devotee, cannot pretend that Nikita's speech was exactly brilliant. But it had far-reaching results. Among those present there were agents of the secret police, who began to make enquiries about the "young comrade from the Helferich-Sade factory," and a few days later detectives called at the office of the factory with a description of the "young comrade." The head engineer, whose name was Levtchenko, was a sympathizer with the left, and, in order that the young workman Khrushchev should not be arrested, he tipped off the heads of all sections. Accordingly, the head of the section in which Nikita was working sent him this brief message: "Clear out."

Nikita cleared out and made his way to Karan in the Donetz basin, near the town of Mariupol. There he managed to get taken on as a turner's mate in a large factory called "The Russian Prudential" which competed with another large factory, the "Nikopol-Mariupolsky." From now on, as his official biography published in Soviet Russia meticulously records, Nikita was "the workman of the Donetz region."

Karan was a very small station on the railway line between Mariupol and the junction at Volnovakha. It consisted of a primitive village containing a few tumble-down cottages near the station. The technicians were accommodated in a large red-brick building, the style of which might be described as 1900 baroque. In front of this building there was a small square.

The manager of the factory, a Belgian Catholic, had an orthodox church built, and appointed a certain Father Vassili as parish priest. He gave orders that workmen should go to Mass on Sundays, attend the confessional regularly and become "exemplary Christians." This was more or less on the lines of the Henry Ford system, as put into operation before the first World War.

The Russian workmen laughed and made jokes about their Belgian manager. Father Vassili, who was fond of vodka, also laughed. The church was attended largely by women who never missed a marriage or a baptism, and there were plenty of these, as the manager "encouraged the faithful" by presenting a gift from the factory to all newly wedded couples and all babies baptized there.

With much difficulty Nikita had found a tiny room in the cottage of a spinster who was the cousin of Pelagia, the priest's wife (Russian orthodox priests are allowed to marry, but not more than once). The spinster was a dear old thing who quickly took to her young boarder and was anxious to "save his soul," for he refused pointblank to set foot in the church. She provided him with a religious magazine edited by the Archbishop of Novotcherkassk. Nikita made no attempt to read these edifying pages, but on the other hand he benefited by the spinster's kindness, for she charged him only one rouble a month for his room.

He found life at Karan dull and dreary after Kharkov. The only amusement was the Sunday program shown at the cinema, or bioscope as it was then called, near the station. The films included such items as "The Flood," "Man and Monkey" and "Cain and Abel." Sometimes comic films were shown, such as "Drenched By His Own Watercan," and the audience then rocked with laughter. Nikita also laughed, for he was a thorough-going Ukrainian in his love of laughter. But the mechanical repetition of the same jokes on the screen soon bored him, and he often went out before the end of the film.

After a year of this existence at Karan he decided to move on, and he went to Mariupol to work in the "Nikopol-Mariupolsky" factory. Mariupol was the chief town of the administrative area. It had its "ispravnik" or sub-prefect of police and 35,000 inhabitants, more than one-third of whom were Greeks. It was an attractive provincial town, situated on the Sea of Azov, at the mouth of the River Kalmius, and it had a theatre, two "bioscopes," a library and a natural history museum.

Nikita found a room and board with a Jewish cobbler named Yankyelyevitch, and he soon became quite a member of the family. On the Sabbath, Jews are forbidden by their religion to light a fire, and Nikita attended to this. Altogether, the Yankyelyevitch family liked their boarder very much, and he picked up enough Yiddish to be able to talk to Khana, his landlady. He also relished Jewish cooking, being particularly fond of stuffed fish, and he received an extra helping of this without any additional charge. It gratified his landlady's Jewish pride to see the young Ukrainian do justice to this typical Jewish dish after the consecration of the Sabbath on Friday evenings.

This was in 1913, at a time when the situation of the Jews in Imperial Russia was lamentable. The Minister of Justice,

Shtcheglovitov, and Maklakov his successor, were rabid anti-Semites, and they had engineered a charge of ritual murder against Beiliss, a Jew at Kiev, who was accused of having killed a Christian boy named Andryusha Yushtchinsky, in order to use his blood for making the unleavened bread eaten by the Jews during the Passover festival. Although this accusation was utterly preposterous, the inhabitants of the Ukraine, the majority of whom were anti-Semites, were convinced that it was true. Rumors of pogroms spread like wildfire throughout the towns of the Jewish pale in Imperial Russia. This pale of settlement included the towns of the Ukraine and Russian Poland (Jews were not allowed to live in the villages), and Mariupol formed part of this ghetto area.

One Friday, when the Jews felt more alarmed than ever (there had been much talk about a pogrom), Nikita did not return at his usual hour. Khana and her husband waited for him anxiously. They recalled the pogrom of 1905 which had claimed so many victims at Mariupol, and they began to wonder whether their boarder was a member of the "Black Hundreds," those gangs of ruffians who went about murdering Jews and raping their wives and daughters.

Suddenly Nikita made his appearance. His face was covered with blood, he had bruises on his forehead and cheeks, and he was limping. Khana was horrified; she bathed his face and applied a wet bandage to his head, where a large lump had already formed as the result of a very severe blow.

"How did this happen, Nikita?"

"I had crossed the market square near the cathedral where a crowd had collected. There were a lot of roughs, dockers, fellows out of work and butchers' apprentices with their knives. Someone was making a speech. When I went closer, I saw that it was Loiko, the butcher, the head of the 'Black Hundred' here."

Khana began to tremble with fear.

"They're going to murder us!" she exclaimed.

"Don't worry," said Nikita. "There's not going to be any pogrom at Mariupol this time."

"Are you sure?" asked the cobbler.

"Yes. While the Loika was speaking, a bunch of our socialist workmen came along, with Leibov the teacher at the head of them. Our fellows were armed with bludgeons and revolvers. Leibov told me they were a detachment of the self-defense corps and asked me to join. So I did, and then there was a bit of a scuffle. Loiko's gang got properly walloped. I was knocked about a bit, too."

The Yankyelyevitch family took an even greater liking to their boarder after his painful encounter with the "Black Hundred."

"He's all right," said the cobbler. "He'll never do us any harm."

Ivan Papadopoulos, a Russified Greek, the director of the natural history museum, had organized an evening class which Nikita attended. Natural history was a subject which greatly interested him. He took lesson notes which he sometimes used to read over during his work at the factory.

He did not remain there for long, however. The board of directors decided to discontinue the section in which he was employed. This marked the beginning of an economic crisis which was making itself felt in Imperial Russia, and which caused many factories to be closed.

Nikita had to go and look for work elsewhere, in places where the effects of the crisis were not so acute. Now began the period in which he became a wanderer, finding his way to nearly every part of the Donetz basin. This made him familiar with all the most important factories, with the mines and workshops, and above all, with the people, the Russian people. Not only did he develop into a "genuine workman of the

Donetz," a "100 per cent proletarian" of this area, the most industrialized part of Imperial Russia, but he also gained an expert knowledge of metallurgy. He acquainted himself, too, with all questions involving the organization of labor and industrial technique. Later on, when he studied at the "Industrial Academies" at Kiev and Moscow, the experiences which he acquired in the Donetz basin stood him in good stead and enabled him to obtain, without any difficulty, a diploma as an "organizing engineer."

At first, Nikita took on a job at Kutchenkovo, but he left this town after three months and worked successively at Gordovka, Yuzovo and Yizdrovka. From there he went to the town of Bakhumut, but he left this place, too, after a short stay. Wages were low and lodgings dear. He made for Yassinovataya, an important railway junction in the Donetz. There he found employment as a turner in the workshop for the repair of railway engines.

Living conditions at Yassinovataya were an improvement on those which he had recently been experiencing. The workmen were accommodated in a large-scale block of buildings, the outcome of a scheme devised by an engineer named Yakovlev, who was in charge of the rolling-stock, and was well known throughout Southern Russia for his liberal ideas. There were apartments with one, two or three rooms, available to the men employed in the repairs workshop.

Nikita had secured a one-room apartment with a kitchen in building V of the block (V, it should be added, is the third letter of the Russian alphabet). He also had a small vestibule, a wall-cupboard in the kitchen and a cellar. Vassia, one of his young cousins who had come from Kharkov to work at Yassinovataya, jokingly said that he had become a regular little bourgeois. Vassia could not find an apartment, and Nikita managed to put him up. He was a year older than Nikita, and had been awarded a certificate at the higher elementary school in Kharkov. He belonged to the revolutionary socialist party, and Nikita took his political cue from Vassia, reading the pamphlets and books which he brought home. He also took part in the heated debates between Vassia and the young people who came to their flat to eat garlic sausage, drink lager beer and discuss the condition of the workers.

In 1914, just before the outbreak of the war, Nikita's fellow-workers had started a sick fund. At this period there was no such thing as social insurance in Russia. The Russian workers, following the example of those in Germany, set up "sick-funds," to which they made voluntary contributions. The socialist parties, which were illegal in Russia (under the terms of the imperial legal code, membership in a socialist party entailed deportation to Siberia), made use of the financial resources derived from these "sick funds" for their propaganda purposes, which they camouflaged as "philanthropic activities." The secret police were well aware of the real nature of these "philanthropic activities," but, as long as they were kept within certain bounds, they were not interfered with.

In 1914 Vassia was elected secretary of the "sick fund," and Nikita became his assistant.

III

THE WAR

Between the spring and the summer of 1914 Russia was in a turmoil.

The process of repressing the revolution of 1905–6 had been completed by Stolypin's "neckties."[1] A reactionary government was adopting retaliatory measures by transforming the Russian peasants, who had been "collectivized" by their "mir," an organization not far short of communism, into small holders, yeomen farmers, on Western lines.

Stolypin, the former governor of Saratov, and undoubtedly one of the Tsar's most able henchmen, understood the peasants thoroughly. He was well aware that their state of abject misery, and particularly the "mir," their communal organization, made it easy for the extremists to achieve their aim of at-

[1] Roditchev, a deputy of the Duma and a member of Milyukov's constitutional party, one day referred to the courts martial set up by Stolypin to quash the insurrection, and he described the gibbets which operated in connection with these courts as "Stolypin's neck-ties". He compared them to the similar arrangements instituted in Poland by Court Muravyev at the time of the insurrection of 1863–4 and known as "Muravyev's collars".

19

tracting the masses of the peasantry to the cause of the social revolution. These masses comprised no less than eighty per cent of the total population of the huge Russian Empire.

By assassinating Stolypin, Bogrov had deprived the Tsar of his chief myrmidon. The reactionary movement did not come to an end, but it had forfeited its ideology and it could now offer the peasants very little. Piotr Arkadyevitch Stolypin, the Tsar's last Boyar, had been replaced by Kokovtsov, a bureaucrat. The extremist parties took advantage of this to get their activities started again.

Between April and July 1914 Russia had become the scene of social disturbances—strikes, armed demonstrations, barricades at St. Petersburg. Raymond Poincaré, the French President, had an opportunity of witnessing this state of affairs when he paid a visit to the Tsar on the eve of the war.

The workmen at Yassinovataya were in a ferment of unrest. Under the pretext of a "general gathering of the members of the sick fund" the delegates of the illegal socialist parties had arranged a regular meeting. There they discussed the possibility of "emphasizing the solidarity of the workers to encourage the St. Petersburg comrades."

Vassia Khrushchev and another revolutionary socialist known as "Zhuk," who had come from St. Petersburg to work at Yassinovataya, organized a strike in the repairs workshop. Their object was to get the railwaymen to stop work, so as to cause a general strike on the Kharkov-Lozovaya-Rostov line. Nikita had taken a hand in this scheme. He did not suspect for a moment that "Zhuk" was an informer of the secret police who had been sent to the Donetz to betray the leaders of the illegal revolutionary socialist movement.

"Zhuk" was a friend of Father Gapon[1] and he must have

---

[1] Father Gapon, born in the village of Lyeshtchinovka, in the administrative area of Poltava, was a picturesque figure in the Russian revolutionary movement. He was the parish priest of a working-class district in St. Peters-

thrown his comrades off the scent when the priest was assassinated.

To be on the safe side, he left St. Petersburg for the Donetz. The activities of "Zhuk" were directed by Captain Vassilyev, of the secret police at Ekaterinoslav (now known as Dnyepropyetrovsk). "Zhuk" received payment for each revolutionary leader arrested, and, in order to discover who they were, he adopted the device of provoking a general strike.

The meeting held by the "sick fund" members was extremely agitated, and the speakers did not mince their words. The first of them was "Zhuk" himself, who insisted on the need for supporting their comrades by means of a general strike. Vassia Khrushchev spoke to the same effect. While they were in the thick of a debate as to how the strike was to be started, Yakovlev, the chief engineer, made his appearance, having been informed by the manager of the "sick-fund" of the real character of the gathering. Yakovlev, who was popular with the workmen, delivered a moving speech. He referred to the "approaching war" and emphasized "the duty of every Russian to defend his country threatened by Germany." The workmen thereupon decided not to start the strike.

Yakovlev then left for Ekaterinoslav, where he asked for an audience with the governor. The latter sent for Captain Vassiliyev, who was responsible for what happened in that particular area. The officer of the secret police now realized what

---

burg, and called himself a "worker-priest" (there is nothing new under the sun) in 1903, in order to organize the trade-union workers who were faithful to the "Little Father, the Tsar, the supreme arbiter in the class struggle in Russia". On January 9th, 1905, Gapon, who was a close friend of Trepov, the governor of St. Petersburg, led a workers' demonstration towards the Winter Palace. This demonstration was fired on by the military and brought to an end. After "Bloody Sunday" Gapon went abroad, where he continued to act as an agent of the secret police among the revolutionaries. On his return to Russia he was assassinated at Terioki by four revolutionary socialists directed by Makar-Rutenberg, who afterwards became a Zionist and helped to build the Jordan dam in Palestine.

a dangerous game his informer was playing, and "Zhuk" was sent to the Urals.[1]

Several of the "ring leaders" were deported to the region of Narym, in Western Siberia, Vassia Khrushchev among them. Nikita, who had not spoken at the meeting, was not interfered with, but he realized that he was a marked man, and he decided to leave Yassinovataya and seek employment in the town of Lugansk (now known as Voroshilovgrad). This was in September 1914, when the war was already raging.

Lugansk was a provincial town, the headquarters of a subprefect of police. It had been built in 1795 by an Englishman named Gascoyne who was invited to Russia to establish a factory for naval aramaments. It was situated on the site of a former Tartar town, Lugan. But it was too far from the sea, and the strange scheme initiated by the ministers of Catherine II to manufacture naval guns there was soon dropped.

In the nineteenth century Lugansk had become an important center for the production of engines and carriages for the Russian railways. The population comprised several thousand workmen, but the climate was unhealthy, owing to the situation of the town in a marshy area, near a stagnant backwater of the Donetz.

It was with some difficulty that Nikita found employment as a turner in a railway-engine factory, but he had no trouble about lodgings. He rented a room on moderate terms from an employee of the excise named Morozov. The events at Kharkov had put him on his guard. He knew that if he attracted the attention of the police in any way he would probably be sent to Siberia. He detested the Tsarist régime, but he was

[1] "Zhuk" was exposed after the revolution when the records of the secret police were examined. He was tried by a people's court at Sverdlovsk (formerly known as Ekaterinenburg) and condemned to death. During the proceedings "Zhuk" gave a full account of his activities in the secret police. Captain Vassiliyev was also tried and was sentenced to ten years' solitary confinement. He asserted that he was not aware that "Zhuk" himself had inspired and organized the meeting.

not particularly anxious to become a martyr. In fact, he was not yet equal to the dangerous activities of a professional revolutionary.

At that time the career of a revolutionary began at the age of eighteen to twenty years. Nikita was just about that age, but he preferred to keep in the background rather than reside in the dismal Siberian tundra. He was affable and light-hearted, fond of amusement and feminine society. He liked going to the theatre, and he was anxious to improve his mind by private study. From his point of view, therefore, it was better to keep out of political mischief.

His work at the factory did not engross him. It was not expected that the war would last long—three or six months at the most. The result was that thousands of specialists had left the factory, and the government had done nothing to ensure an increased rate of output.

Nikita was due to begin his military service in 1915, on reaching his twentieth year. Thus, until the autumn of 1915 he still had one more year at his disposal. He took full advantage of it. Vladimir Andriyevsky, whose book was quoted in an earlier chapter, and who was now studying at the Agricultural College in Kharkov,[1] saw Nikita in 1914. Andriyevsky gives an account of their meeting at Kharkov, where Nikita had gone "to relax" from his work in the factory at Lugansk.

"I met him," says Andriyevsky, "in a large beerhall near the station. He was with two young ladies whom he introduced to me as his cousins."

Andriyevsky goes on to say that Nikita was dressed in a manner which, by the standards of the Kharkov working classes, was considered smart. He wore a grey woollen cap, a dark blue coat of diagonal cloth made at Lodz, light blue, bell-bottomed trousers, all the rage among the Odessa toughs who

[1] Before the war this college was at Novo-Alexandria, near Lublin, but it was evacuated to Kharkov in September 1914.

had copied them from the sailors, and now an essential item in the uniform of the Russian proletarian dandies.

He evidently had plenty of money to spend. He kept urging his friends to order "another bottle." He himself was drinking beer. Now and then he cautiously took a bottle of vodka out of his trousers pocket, and after sipping at it, put it back with equal caution.[1]

"My favorite drink is yorsh,"[2] he declared gleefully. "Beer's all right for Germans. But vodka's the stuff for Russians."

"Aren't you afraid of getting tight?" I asked him.

Nikita burst out laughing.

"Not me," he replied. "I'm a 'luzhenny.' 'Yorsh' has no effect on me."

"And he was right," continues Andriyevsky. "I saw him swill five bottles of beer and a bottle of vodka, Smirnov 56, without batting an eyelid."

"Why," Nikita went on, "I could take on Dobromysslov at this game."

(Dobromysslov, it should be explained, was a Kharkov merchant who established a record at a drinking competition by accounting for ten bottles of beer and more than two pints of vodka 56.)

"At this moment," says Andriyevsky, "a big, fat man of about fifty-five to sixty, came up to us. He looked at Nikita with a touch of contempt.

"'You young whipper-snapper,' he remarked. 'You'd take on Dobromysslov, would you? Why, he's the city champion.

---

[1] The drinking of vodka was prohibited in the Russian beerhalls. Heavy fines were inflicted, not only on any customer infringing this order, but also on the proprietor of the establishment.

[2] "Yorsh" is a mixture of beer and vodka which is very intoxicating. It was a "point of honor" with Russian drinkers who took themselves seriously to brew a portion of "yorsh" by mixing about six pints of beer and a pint and a half of vodka 56. A drinker who could stand this mixture with impunity was called "luzhenny," which may be rendered approximately as "armor-plated."

You come here tomorrow. I'm Dobromysslov's cousin, and I wager you won't be able to drink more than me. And let me tell you, compared with my cousin, I'm just a beginner, as you might say.' "

"That was my last meeting with Nikita," adds Andriyevsky. "I don't know whether he went to the 'New Bavaria' beer-hall the next day, and whether he held his own with the cousin of the 'Kharkov Champion.' "

In the summer of 1915 the Tsarist government had become aware that it would be a fatal mistake to squander the factory specialists, and a decree was issued to the effect that turners and turners' mates were not to be called to the colors if they were working in the war industry or in connection with the transport system.

Nikita Khrushchev was now in a safe job. He could not be called up for the army. His wages were steadily increasing. He could afford to eat and drink to his heart's content. But we have few details of the life of Khrushchev during this period. In 1938, however, the *Voroshilovgrad News* published an article by a certain Kotov, from which we learn that Nikita had become a great reader. He took out a subscription with the Popular Library at Lugansk which entitled him to borrow five books at a time. He seems to have covered a very wide ground, for, according to Kotov, who was the librarian, he took out works by Gogol, Pushkin, Lermontov, Goncharov, Spielhagen, Zola, Balzac, Goethe, Maupassant, Dickens, Nekrassov and Schiller. In addition to these authors, he read all the available popular books on science. One book which he kept for quite a long time was *Force and Matter* by the German writer Georg Büchner, which was a prime favorite with the Russians before the revolution.

Nikita also attended evening classes, pretentiously called "The Popular University," at which a few lecturers taught mathematics, science, spelling, history and geography. He thus profited by the period of the war to give himself some sort of education, and, as he had ability, the evening classes were of great use to him.

Kotov, who besides being a librarian, taught spelling at these classes, tells us that Khrushchev easily mastered the oddities of Russian spelling, which were apt to puzzle even well-educated persons before the reform of 1917. Thus, towards 1917, the year of the revolution, Nikita was no longer the illiterate youngster whom we first encountered at Kalinovka.

IV

THE REVOLUTION BREAKS OUT

The revolution of February 1917 (March, according to the Western calendar) broke out in an unexpected manner. The ground had been prepared for it by that complete disintegration of the imperial ruling class which formed a sequel to the Rasputin scandal, but the actual outbreak was caused by a revolt of the working-class women when no bread was obtainable in Petrograd. At the same time, it was facilitated by the fact that Petrograd was crowded with disaffected soldiers, the result being that within one week the feudal Russian Empire was transformed into the super-democratic republic of Prince Lvov and Kerensky.

Nikita Khrushchev, like millions of others, was thrilled by the news of the revolution. He promptly left Lugansk and went to Kharkov, where his relatives again let him have a room free of charge. He had no difficulty in finding employment in the railway-engine factory there.

At this juncture, Kharkov was seething with revolutionary enthusiasm. The city was gay with flags, and the two largest squares—the Nikolayevskaya and the Pavovskaya—were packed with people, who, chewing sunflower seeds, eagerly listened to speeches by orators of various parties. Some of these speeches were ridiculous in the extreme, but they were wildly applauded nevertheless. The Russian people, hitherto condemned to silence, was now indulging in a frenzy of talk.

Nikita also delivered a speech now and then. In 1937 the newspaper *Trud* contained an article by a certain Kruglov, who at that time was working in the same factory as Nikita. He described a meeting held on the large square in front of the southern railway station, where a huge crowd had collected. Nikita's speech followed that of a delegate of the provisional government. This was the period when Professor Milyukov, the minister of foreign affairs, had sent a diplomatic note to the Allies, urging that the Straits should be granted to Russia in return for her participation in the war. Milyukov was simple-minded enough to imagine that such a concession would help the government to convince the soldiers that the war must be continued. His speech had quite a different effect. The extremists exploited it to accuse the provisional government of wanting "to shed the blood of the people in an imperialist cause."

"Comrade Khrushchev," says Kruglov in his article, "spoke for the purpose of exposing the real aim of the imperialist Milyukov." In a short but vehement speech Nikita explained that the "cadets," the name given to the members of Milyukov's party, wanted to continue the war to enrich themselves and help the makers of munitions to enrich themselves also. The workers and peasants would gain nothing by the annexation of the Straits.

Suddenly some Cossacks, part of a detachment on its way to the front, appeared on the scene. The officer in charge of them was an aggressive young lieutenant. He climbed on to the rostrum and tried to make Comrade Khrushchev get down. This led to a scuffle, in which the workmen and the railway-men from the station came to Nikita's help. Thus, in 1917 he figured as what was called an "internationalist," but he was not yet a bolshevik.

At that time Lenin and his party had not yet monopolized internationalism, nor were they the sole representatives of Russian "revolutionary democracy." Another party, young and energetic, calling itself the party of "the left-wing revolutionary socialists," had now come into being, in opposition to Lenin and his followers.

Nikita, although filled with "internationalist" sentiments, was far more attracted by the new party than by Lenin's bolsheviks. He attended their meetings, at which he spoke as "Comrade Nikita," but he was in no hurry to have himself enrolled as an effective member of the party.

Meanwhile he was to be seen having a good time in the various haunts of amusement, the dance halls of the suburb in which he was living, the theatres which specialized in vaudeville and musical comedy. With the fustian smartness of his attire, his auburn hair and engaging expression, Nikita, the future first secretary of the communist party of the Soviet Union, was the pet of the young ladies in the "Cold Hill" district of Kharkov.

In August 1917 General Kornilov, elbowed into dictatorship by an adventurer named Zavoiko and a few self-seekers, started his revolt against Kerensky, and the left-wing revolutionary socialists held a number of meetings at Kharkov in opposition to Kornilov. But Nikita attended none of them. He had left Kharkov to spend a month with his mother and the rest of the family at Kalinovka.

The peasants were now beginning to share out the land, without awaiting the decision of the constituent assembly. This was a movement which made a very strong appeal to Nikita, with his peasant origin, and he was elected chairman of the "Distribution Committee" at Kalinovka. This was the first position of rank which he held in the new Russia. He set about his work with gusto. A list of the peasants in the commune, with the members of their families, had been drawn up, and the land had been classified into several categories. Careful calculation had been made of the share per person and of the coefficient of productivity of each category of land.

After having completed all these formalities, Nikita saw to it that the "Distribution Committee" adopted the system of distribution which he had devised. This was in October 1917, just one month before the bolshevist revolution. Nikita now left Kalinovka and returned to Kharkov, and from there he went to Lugansk. It is not quite clear why he went back to the Donetz region, but it may fairly be conjectured that he did so for personal reasons. One of his girl cousins had joined the bolshevist party and had left Kharkov for Lugansk. This was his favorite cousin, and it is highly probable that he had gone to join her.

When the November revolution broke out, he was a turner and fitter in a metal works. Lugansk had become the "personal fief" of Klementi Efremovitch Voroshilov, the president of the town soviet. Voroshilov, an "old bolshevik," was, at bottom, merely a revolutionary trouble-maker. Before the revolution he had attended the congress at London and also the conference at Hammerfors, where he had made the acquaintance of Lenin.

Voroshilov's speeches in the soviet were vehement and fiery, but they were far from being "Marxist," although Klim, as he was generally called, did his level best to convince his audience that he was a "revolutionary Marxist" (such, by the way, was Trotsky's opinion). That is perhaps why his speeches made such a deep impression on that "left-wing revolutionary socialist," Nikita Khrushchev. This meeting of his with Klim Voroshilov, who, according to Trotsky, was "a revolutionary democrat masquerading as a Marxist bolshevik," influenced Nikita more than all the speeches of the Kharkov bolsheviks, who talked about "the general line of the revolutionary Marxist."

In December 1917 Nikita was elected a member of the Lugansk soviet, on which he was appointed deputy-head of the military section. This body was concerned with the recruiting of detachments of Red Guards who were fighting against the Don Cossacks and Kaledin, their ataman. Nikita commanded a detachment of Red Guards who were defending Rostov against the Cossacks, and he also fought against the Whites at Rutchenkovo, Yuzovo, Gorlovka, Pavolgrad, Melitopol and a number of other places. He took part in the Battle of Taganrog, in which a few hundred "yunkers," or cadets of the military academy, managed to defeat a large detachment of Red Guards. Nikita was wounded in this battle and evacuated to Lugansk, where he spent more than three months in the hospital.

When he left the hospital in March 1918, the Germans were advancing from Kiev to Kharkov. Marshal von Mackensen, their commander-in-chief, had received orders to occupy the whole of the Ukraine as a source of food supplies. The Reich was being strangled by the Allied blockade. The Red government of Kiev had fled before the German cavalry, which was advancing on the Kiev-Bakhmatch-Sumy-Kharkov line. Klim Voroshilov, appointed commander-in-chief of the Red Guards of the Ukraine, had drawn up his "plan." He wanted to obtain an assurance from the Germans that the Kharkov-Lugansk-Mariupol area should not form part of the Ukraine, in return for a promise that Klim would not interfere with the German rear. This area would then be governed by a "directoire," under the charge of Emmanuel Kviring, a bolshevik.[1] This new area was to be known as the "Tsikedon-

[1] He was shot by Yezhov in 1938, at the time of the Great Purge.

krivbass." Marshal von Eichhorn, who had been appointed governor general at Kiev (he spoke Russian extremely well), roared with laughter when he was told about Klim's "geographical brainwave," which he described as "Russian moonshine."

Thereupon Voroshilov decided to meet the Germans in battle near Kharkov. He assembled all his detachments, amounting to about 30,000 men. The Germans had an overwhelming superiority, their numerical strength being 100,000, including abundant artillery, aircraft and armored trains. The Red Guards were defeated. Nikita took part in this battle as commander of the "First proletarian regiment of the Donbass." This was a high rank for a man who had never performed his regular military service. Retreating before the German cavalry, Nikita's regiment withdrew to Kharkov. There it became necessary to put down a civilian upheaval and counter the onslaughts of Sadovsky's detachment, organized for "the self-defense of the population." Kharkov had become the scene of violence and looting by assorted gangs of thugs.

Nikita had an expert knowledge of Kharkov, and he succeeded in leading a detachment through the city and occupying its well-to-do areas. The German cavalry, the fifth regiment of Bavarian uhlans, entered Kharkov by way of the "Cold Hill" district, and were held up for a whole day by Nikita's regiment. When the last Red trains had left the Bakhmut station (the eastern terminus), Nikita issued the order for the evacuation of Kharkov, and his regiment began to retreat towards Byelgorod. There, Nikita signed an application for enrollment in the bolshevik party. This was in April 1918. He had just turned twenty-four. He had now ceased to waver. A new career was beginning for him, a career which was to make Nikita the successor of Lenin and Stalin as head of the communist party of Soviet Russia.

V

THE START OF A CAREER

And so in April 1918 Nikita Khrushchev became an effective member of Lenin's party. At first, he remained with his regiment in the Byelgorod area, near the new Russian-Rumanian frontier, established under the terms of the Treaty of Brest-Litovsk. But the Donetz proletarians who had joined the army to fight in defense of the Ukraine had no desire to putter about as frontier guards. Little by little they slipped away. Nikita had applied for a transfer to the party committee at Kursk. He wanted to be sent to Moscow to study agriculture.

His application was rejected. The First Donbass regiment was disbanded, and its commanding officer was appointed head of the agricultural department at Kursk. The duties of this department were to put the agrarian reform into operation. Nikita's experience with the "Distribution Committee" was a great asset to him and he proved extremely efficient in his new post. When he came to Moscow with his report for the agricultural commission, the director, Kalyegayeff, congratulated him and mentioned his name to Lenin, for it was he who, having a special interest in agrarian reform, had asked Khrushchev to make a report to the council of people's commissaries. This brought Nikita into personal touch with Lenin, or Ilyitch, as he was known in party circles.

In 1939, on the fifteenth anniversary of Lenin's death, he said that Lenin had made an unforgettable impression on him. "Lenin," he remarked, "was unpretentious and easily accessible. He listened with close attention to everything I told him." When he mentioned these details he could never have imagined that, some thirty years after the death of Ilyitch, he himself would be appointed head of the Russian communist party, "the first among the equals," just as Lenin was.

On his return to Kursk, Nikita found that the party had selected him for a new post. He was to be head of the "extraordinary commission" on the frontier. He was just beginning to enter upon his official duties when Germany collapsed beneath the blows of the Entente, and Lenin annulled the Treaty of Brest-Litovsk. Troops of Soviet Russia invaded the Ukraine, where a general insurrection had overthrown the government of Skoropadsky the hetman.

Khrushchev was transferred to Kharkov with special authority to handle important legal matters, and he held this post until May 1919. He worked in a department dealing with what was described as "the struggle against crime," and in particular against the seditious and nationalistic risings among the Ukrainian peasantry. These risings, sponsored by the moderate Ukrainian parties and the famous Ataman Makhno, an anarchist, had assumed alarming proportions, and the troops of the "extraordinary commission" had to wage continual guerilla warfare.

In the spring of 1919 the White Army of General Denikin began its offensive against the Reds in the Ukraine. General

May-Mayevsky, commander of the seasoned divisions of Markhov, Drozdovsky and Kornilov, had defeated the Reds in the Donetz. He was advancing swiftly towards Kharkov, erecting gibbets for the communists along his route.

Nikita left for the front as commander of the "special battalion." Near the station of Lozovaya his troops were decimated by the White cavalry of General Schiffner-Markevitch. The Reds who survived fled in desperation, for they knew that the Whites relentlessly hanged all the Red troops whom they caught. Nikita managed to escape from the trap into which they had fallen, and as a result of which they were encircled. Disguised as a peasant, he wandered about for more than a fortnight until he reached the large forest of Babtchany, near Tchuguyev, where a detachment of the Reds had taken refuge.

The partisan war now began in the Ukraine. Khrushchev, who had been promoted to political commissar of the detachment, had shown that he was a fearless leader. The blood of the Zaporog Cossacks was asserting itself. His detachment sometimes came out of the forest, under cover of night, to attack the townships and villages occupied by the Whites. As soon as a village was taken, the White prisoners were shot, frequently in the very place where a gibbet had been erected for the Red prisoners hanged on the previous day. The civil war was waged with the utmost ruthlessness, but Nikita quickly became accustomed to its savagery. "Kill or be killed" was the slogan of both sides in this fratricidal struggle.

The Red partisans did exercise some semblance of justice in the form of a court for trying the Whites, and Nikita, the political commissar, acted also as prosecutor. His severity became proverbial. His indictments and speeches were pitiless. At that particular period neither the Reds nor the Whites, when trying men during the civil war, troubled to treat each individual case on its merits. "The mad dogs of capitalism

always deserve death." That was the attitude adopted by the
Reds, and the three judges reached their decisions promptly,
after which the executions were carried out there and then.
When the Reds fell into the hands of the Whites, similar
"justice" was meted out to the "Red rabble," the only differ-
ence being that a gibbet took the place of a firing squad.

Nikita was not cruel by temperament, but the habit of
shedding blood and running the risk each day of being
hanged on a telegraph pole (for after a while the Whites no
longer troubled to erect gibbets, the winter being cold and
wood in short supply) had made him callous to the sufferings
of the White prisoners. "Khrushch" (for he was called by the
name of his Cossack ancestors) was considered to be a holy
terror by the Ukrainian partisans who infested the woods, and
their leaders were often as ferocious as the Atamans Gonta
and Yelezniak who slaughtered the whole population of the
town of Uman in the eighteenth century.

When the Whites were defeated at Tula, Orel and Voronezh in the winter of 1919–20, the partisans came out of the
forest to join the regular forces of the Red Army and to occupy Kharkov. In January 1920 Trotsky, the commander-in-
chief of the Red Army, arrived at Kharkov. An elaborate
military review to celebrate the victory was arranged. Trotsky
delivered one of his fiery speeches and distributed orders of
the "Red Flag," the only military distinction which existed at
that time.

The Pavlovsky Square, opposite the headquarters of the
Ukrainian central executive committee, was crowded with
soldiers and civilians. In the middle of the square a platform
had been set up, and on it Trotsky, surrounded by the men in
charge of the Soviet Ukraine, made a speech before distribut-
ing the decorations. He said:

"Kharkov is like a radish, red outside and white inside.
When our armies left your city in 1919 the inhabitants fired

on the Red Army. Even the proletarians of Kharkov did not give full support to the Soviet government. There was only one small group which defended the city of Kharkov to the last against the hordes of German imperialism. The First proletarian regiment of the Donetz was the one which saved the proletarian honor of your city, which has become once again an honest Soviet city. Glory to that regiment! Glory to its First battalion which held out at Kharkov to the last."

The "Red Carnot" then went on to declare that the Soviet government at Moscow had decided to award a "flag of honor" to the First proletarian regiment and to bestow the order of the "Red Flag" on the battalion commanders.

A march past then began, and when it was over Trotsky read out the names of those who were to be decorated:

". . . Nikita Khrushchev . . ."

Nikita mounted the platform and Trotsky pinned on his chest the first military order instituted as a result of the November revolution in Soviet Russia.

Nikita's detachment was disbanded, and some of the partisans were enrolled in the regular army. He himself was offered the rank of commanding officer if he cared to remain in the Red Army, but he refused. He was not keen on a military career, and he applied for demobilization with a view to completing his studies. He was now twenty-six years of age, but he nevertheless felt delighted when he was informed by the party committee that he was going to be sent to attend a workers' educational course to study agriculture, side by side with young people scarcely out of their teens.

The students were accommodated in a hostel at Kharkov. It was a dilapidated house, devoid of windowpanes or proper plumbing, and its walls were caked with dirt. They came from all parts of Russia, tired of war and eager for education. Very soon, the gaping windows were stuffed with sheets of cardboard, a huge latrine was dug in the courtyard, and the walls were white-washed. The place was made habitable again.

The young students, both men and women, shared the three stories of the house. The standards of conduct in the hostel were simple and free from pretense—free, too, from the promiscuity which was rife in other places where young students were living at this chaotic period. Love-affairs nearly always led to a regular marriage in a register office, and the comrades then organized a "marriage banquet" by pooling their meager rations.

Nikita, too, had a love affair at the hostel, and one day in the spring of 1922 he married a Miss Surkova, who was also studying agriculture. There were three children of this marriage, a daughter and two sons, one of whom, an airman, was killed in the last war. Nikita and his wife soon left the hostel, and by means of wire-pulling he obtained a small flat. His marriage made no change in his educational plans. He had already attracted the attention of his teachers by a number of essays on his special subject, and one of these essays, which dealt with the rotation of crops in the Kursk area, brought him in a prize of a hundred roubles. With the help of his wife Nikita had made up his mind to write a book on the rotation of crops throughout the Ukraine. He spent much time in the library of the Agricultural College, while his wife was to have helped him by her research work at the experimental station. It is probable that Nikita would have become a distinguished agricultural expert if a new political situation had not arisen at Kharkov and in Soviet Russia as a whole. Trotsky had started his struggle against Stalin. The young students dropped their educational work and threw themselves resolutely into the struggle. Nikita, too, adopted this course. Why was he opposed to Trotsky? Why did he become one of those few students who violently criticized the commander-in-chief, denouncing his "deviations" and "errors"?

One of his fellow-students, named Lazarev, left some reminiscences of that period, which were published in 1938 in the *Kiev News,* a Ukrainian paper. He wrote as follows:

". . . Comrade Khrushchev soon realized that Trotsky was nothing but a menshevik, and a traitor to boot. Trotsky's ideology reeked of class treachery, counter-revolution and the restoration of capitalism in Soviet Russia. Comrade Khrushchev was one of those who were able to convince their fellow-students that Trotskyism was dishonest and treacherous, and he did not hesitate to say so in 1923, at a time when the Trotskyists exerted great influence upon the bulk of the students."

The reminiscences of Lazarev are written in the style of the out-and-out Stalinism of 1938, and they do not supply an answer to the question: Why did Nikita become an anti-Trotskyist? They merely inform us that he had the great courage which was needed to stem the tide of opinion among the students.

In 1923 Trotsky was still the commander-in-chief of the Red Army. Nobody could foretell who would emerge triumphant from the struggle between him and the Stalin-Zinovyev-Kamenyev triumvirate. In 1924, when Lazar Kaganovitch, the new secretary-general of the Ukrainian communist party, arrived at Kharkov, the students were almost completely won over to Trotskyism. Kaganovitch had been appointed by Stalin as his personal representative in the Ukraine to combat Trotskyism, but, in spite of Stalin's support, Kaganovitch had many difficulties to contend with. He was particularly handicapped by his Jewish origin; anti-Semitism was very strong in the Ukraine, even in the very heart of the communist party. On one occasion Kaganovitch came to attend a gathering of Nikita's fellow-students, and he had to cope with an audience completely out of hand. There was a regular spate of Trotskyist speeches.

Only one student ventured to oppose this welter of Trotskyism by making an impassioned speech in favor of the "general line," in favor of Stalin. He was booed and hissed, and all manner of missiles were flung at him. But he stood his ground, finished his speech, and succeeded in gaining several dozen votes in support of his motion.

"What is the name of that student?" asked Kaganovitch.

"Nikita Khrushchev," was the answer.

The next day, the secretary-general of the Ukrainian communist party sent for Nikita. Kaganovitch asked him a number of questions about his past record, his social origins and his present activities. He was satisfied with the answers which he received, and said to Nikita:

"You must give up your studies. We need propagandists like you, young, go-ahead, and of proletarian origin, who have themselves been manual workers. It's with people of your kind that we've got to fight Trotsky's menshevism."

Kaganovitch had been a working tanner and was proud of his social background. He was anxious to gather round him "hundred per cent proletarians," and Nikita was exactly the kind of helper he wanted, for the "workers of the Donetz" were the most genuine proletarians in the Ukraine. This, then, was the way in which Nikita became the propagandist of the central committee of the party.

VI

NIKITA'S CAREER UNDERGOES VICISSITUDES

The propagandist of the central committee proved to be as live a wire in his new post as he had been when on the land distribution committee, the extraordinary commission, in the army and in the forest of Babtchany. He was seething with energy. Every day he delivered five to ten speeches. He was more than a match for all opposition, and he did not mind if it was accompanied by threats. He used to begin his speeches by saying:

"I am a proletarian of the Donetz."

These words always did the trick, for the social origins of the majority of the students in his audience were more or less "dubious."

Every evening he would call at the office of the secretary-general, which looked out on to the grounds of the University. Kaganovitch was always satisfied with the reports which Nikita submitted, and he had every reason to be. He was now provided with an untiring propagandist who could argue

with equal facility about the Erfurt program, the Gotha program, the communist manifesto, or the integral dogma of
Marx's *Das Kapital.* On several occasions Nikita, self-taught
though he was, had beaten the professors of Marxist dialectics
at their own game during debates on a subject of some considerable importance. The point at issue was whether the establishment of socialism was possible in one single country,
Soviet Russia. The Trotskyists asserted that Stalin had made
a gross blunder as regards orthodox Marxism, by enunciating
the principle of the "establishment of socialism in one single
country." There were abundant proofs of this blunder, they
said. Nearly every article by Marx and Engels mentioned
"world-wide revolution" as an "essential condition" for the
establishment of socialism.

The pundits were in a quandary. It was all very well to re-
fute Trotsky at popular gatherings and meetings of workers,
by means of more or less faked quotations. But they could
hardly risk that with the Marxist intellectuals, students and
university men. One day Nikita, after having quietly listened
to Professor Krassner, the exponent of Trotskyism at Kharkov, spoke up. He said:

"I am not a professor. I am only a proletarian of the Donetz.
But I urge Comrade Krassner to be good enough to read
carefully the appendix to the Gotha program of the German
social democrats, drawn up personally by Friedrich Engels."

And taking a notebook from his pocket, Nikita read a long
and tortuous sentence, from which it could be deduced that
the establishment of socialism in one single country is possible "in the determined historical conditions and circumstances." Instead of asking for an elucidation of this sentence, Krassner rapped out, for Nikita's benefit:

"That's a fake, concocted by Stalin."

Thereupon the propagandist of the central committee tri-
umphantly produced from an inside pocket a book published

at Moscow in 1921 and containing a preface by Trotsky. It was a history of the working-class movement in Germany, and it confirmed verbatim the sentence which Nikita had read. The wily Ukrainian had foreseen that his opponents would accuse him of quoting faked evidence and he had prepared a reply accordingly. The book was passed round among the audience. There could not be the slightest doubt about it. Trotsky, their idol, had written a preface to a book in which the Gotha program was reproduced, involving the conclusion that the Stalinist thesis is correct.

The younger generation of Soviet students, who had been trained to foster a fetishist cult of Marx, Lenin and Engels, were dumbfounded by this overwhelming proof. It was almost as if, at a eucharistic congress, someone had produced an item of evidence written by the Apostle Peter. For the first time since the struggle against the opposition at Kharkov, a meeting of students had turned down the Trotskyist motion.

Nikita's success was phenomenal. He was promoted to deputy head of the propaganda section of the central committee of the party. Henceforward he no longer had to attend meetings in person. He directed a "team of propagandists." He drew up instructions. He elaborated theses. This work was extremely congenial to him. The light in his office could be seen burning until the early hours of the morning. He was already being spoken of as a "rising star" in the provisional capital of the Ukraine.[1]

Suddenly the situation changed. Kaganovitch was recalled to Moscow by Stalin, and the leadership of the party was transferred to Skrypnik, an old bolshevik, a Ukrainian patriot and a member of the politbureau. The new secretaries of the central committee, Postyshev, Kossior and Lebed, were not of sufficient caliber to oppose the "Ukrainization" which

[1] Kharkov became the provisional capital of the Ukraine in 1920 during the war with Poland, Polish troops having occupied Kiev in May 1920.

Skrypnik demanded. From now onwards all the leading members of the party and the functionaries of the central committee had to be able to speak and write Ukrainian, and to make public speeches in that language.

Nikita Khrushchev, the descendant of the Zaporog Cossacks, came to grief as a result of Skrypnik's "Ukrainization" policy. At first sight this may seem paradoxical, but the fact is that the people of the Ukraine, especially in the administrative area of Kursk, did not speak Ukrainian. What they spoke was a hodgepodge of Russian and Ukrainian, containing turns of phrase which were so peculiar that it was difficult to understand them. Such, at least, was the linguistic situation as far as the peasantry was concerned.

In Imperialist Russia the Kursk area had never formed part of the administrative region of the Ukraine when a governor general was first appointed there, and at the present time Kursk is in the Russian federative republic, and not in the Ukraine at all. A former Soviet diplomat, Gregor Bessedovsky, who "chose freedom" in 1930, fifteen years before Kravtchenko, has given a very graphic account of the conditions there in the 'twenties in his *Memoirs of a Soviet Diplomat*. Bessedovsky, who was a member of the central executive committee of the Ukraine and a personal friend of Skrypnik, says:

I came into contact with quite a number of functionaries of the central committee of the party at Kharkov. Nearly all of them were dismayed at the thought of having to learn Ukrainian if they were to retain their posts. What struck me particularly was the fact that many of these functionaries, though of Ukrainian origin, did not know our language and had no desire to learn it.

Before joining the communist party, I was a member of the Ukrainian socialist party, which advocated a rapid Ukrainization of government and party in the Ukraine. For my own amusement I deliberately used to speak Ukrainian to the Russian bureaucrats sent by Moscow to Kharkov, and to witness their lam-

entable attempts to carry on a conversation in Ukrainian. They
floundered about in a preposterous gibberish, neither Russian nor
Ukrainian.

Among those members of the central committee who were of
Ukrainian origin, but who had not succeeded in learning their
native language, I came across a certain Khrushchev, from Kursk.
Although he was the propagandist of the central committee, he
could not speak Ukrainian. One day he made a speech before a
group of commissars for foreign affairs, whose permanent secretary, Nikolas Lyubtchenko, was a well-known Ukrainian author.
Khrushchev had, of course, spoken in Russian, and after his
speech Lyubtchenko rose and said:

"Before discussing the question dealt with by Comrade Krush-
chev, I will give you a Ukrainian translation of his speech."

Khrushchev, the self-taught student, had learnt to speak
correct Russian, but in spite of all his efforts he had failed to
speak correct Ukrainian. As Bessedovsky emphasizes, this was
a serious shortcoming for a man who was head of the propaganda section, since propaganda included the policy of
Ukrainization. Skrypnik, a testy and cantankerous person,
promptly mentioned the matter to the politbureau. On one
occasion he had paid a personal call at the propaganda office
and made a long statement to Nikita in Ukrainian. When
Nikita began his reply, Skrypnik at once interrupted him. He
exclaimed:

"It is a disgrace for the head of the propaganda section to
speak Ukrainian so badly, especially when he is a Ukrainian.
Don't you want to learn our language? Why, you're nothing
but a Russianizer."

Khrushchev flushed with anger, but he could not start an
argument with Skrypnik, who, at this period, was Stalin's
"man," successfully fighting against Trotskyism in the
Ukraine.

Nikita, however, has a long memory, and when in 1934 he
became the secretary of the party committee at Moscow, close

to Kaganovitch and Molotov, and known to Stalin personally, he did all he could to settle his accounts with Skrypnik, the "national deviationist." But this time, the "national deviationists" were already under fire, and Skrypnik had been summoned to Moscow to "vindicate himself" at a plenary session of the central committee of the communist party. There, Nikita went for him, tooth and nail. This for example, is a short specimen of his onslaught, transcribed from the shorthand records of the proceedings on that occasion:

"You are a jingo, a traitor. Weren't you one of those who urged that the Cyrillic alphabet should be replaced by the Latin alphabet in the Ukraine?[1] That is rank treason. Pilsudski is in favor of the same scheme. That means that you're nothing but a Polish agent."

Skrypnik was severely reprimanded and removed from the central committee. Knowing that, before long, he would be expelled from the party, and arrested by the GPU, he committed suicide in his apartment at the National Hotel.

Nikita's revenge was complete.

However, this did not happen until 1934, and we are still concerned with events in 1928, when Nikita was only a functionary of the central committee, whereas Skrypnik was one of the most influential members of the politbureau. Nikita, therefore, had to pocket the insult and hold his tongue. He did so, and he did not remain much longer in the propaganda section. He forestalled his dismissal by asking to be relieved of his duties, under the pretext that he was anxious "to study industrial organization at the Kiev Industrial Academy."

Stanislas Kossior, who greatly appreciated Nikita's work, tried to retain him on the central committee as head of the chancellery. But Nikita refused point-blank, and he was sent

---

[1] The Ukrainians use practically the same Cyrillic alphabet as the Russians, with some additional letters of their own. In Galicia, where many Ukrainians live, the Polish government wanted to replace the Cyrillic alphabet, as used by them, with the Latin alphabet, as used by the Poles.

to the Industrial Academy with an authorization from the central committee of the party and an extremely flattering testimonial from the staff section. It read as follows:

"A staunch party member. Thoroughly familiar with the theory of Marxism. A good orator. Keeps strictly and unswervingly to the general line. Proved his worth during the struggle against opposition. High standard of general knowledge."

The communist cell at the Kiev Industrial Academy received the new student with open arms. The students there formed a non-Ukrainian majority, comprising Russians, Poles and Jews. The Ukrainization policy had not yet affected this cell. Nikita was quickly promoted to head of the organizing section of the cell bureau.

The Kiev Industrial Academy had more than 3,000 students, and the membership of the party communist cell was about 800. It formed one of the most important cells at Kiev. His duties were to select instructors and to test them before they were sent to factories and other important organizations; to carry out purges among those whose social origins were "dubious"; and to draw up a scheme of work. Here, as head of the organizing section, Nikita was thoroughly in his element. Though exacting and strict, he was able to maintain the spirit of comradeship with his fellow-workers. He never took advantage of his position to gain personal benefits such as a better apartment, a privileged food ration, a few extra yards of cloth, and so on. He was simple, unassuming, cheerful and affable. If a discussion became too heated, he would cut it short with a proverb, a joke or an apt anecdote. This was rare among the men who were in charge of departments and who were apt to be devoid of any human quality. It was this quality which Nikita possessed in a very high degree, and he quickly became popular.

Nevertheless he was not satisfied with his work. The policy

of Ukrainization was now becoming rampant everywhere and it had reached the Industrial Academy. The percentage of Ukrainians among the students was steadily on the increase, and the Ukrainian language was heard more and more. Nikita realized that, sooner or later, he would find himself in the same predicament as when he was in the propaganda section of the central committee, and he therefore wrote to Kaganovitch at Moscow.

He asked to be recalled to Moscow, for the purpose of completing his studies at the Industrial Academy there, known as the Joseph Stalin Academy. At the end of 1929 the central committee of the Russian communist party instructed the party committee at Kiev to send Nikita Khrushchev to Moscow for the reasons which he had indicated in his application.

VII

AT MOSCOW

In 1930 Nikita arrived in Moscow with his wife and children to enroll at the Industrial Academy. Before going to the Academy he called on Kaganovitch, who was both secretary of the party committee for the Moscow area and third secretary of the central committee of the communist party. The struggles against the Trotskyists were now over. The "leftists" had been defeated. Now another struggle was beginning, this time against the "rightists," Rykov, Bukharin, Tomsky, Piatakov and Sokolnikov. This struggle was to prove more dangerous to Stalin than that against the "leftists." Rykov, the former president of the council, had a very large number of friends in all the ministries. Bukharin had a considerable following in the very core of the party and among the younger generation, while Tomsky had tremendous influence with the trade-union workers. Piatakov and Sokolnikov had, for a long time, been in charge of the finances and industry of Soviet Russia.

The "rightists" were backed by nearly the whole of the

Soviet bureaucracy, a new privileged stratum which had been created by Stalin as part of his "socialism in one single country," and which was already threatening to replace the dictatorship of the politbureau with that of the "Soviet technocrats."

Stalin had placed Kaganovitch in charge of the Moscow party committee for the purpose of keeping Moscow under control. Uglanov, his predecessor, had compromised himself by a number of secret deliberations with the "rightists." Stalin needed an absolutely reliable henchman, and Kaganovitch gave him every guarantee of fulfilling this requirement.

Kaganovitch, again, needed helpers to occupy secretarial positions in Moscow and its environs. Uglanov's men were still well entrenched in these positions, and they would have to be tracked down and eliminated.

Kaganovitch already knew exactly the kind of man Nikita was. He had seen the work which he had done, and was entirely satisfied with him as a "proletarian of the Donetz," a "well-trained Marxist" and a "staunch party member." He therefore quickly reached a decision. He would keep Khrushchev for a time at the head of the cell in the Moscow Industrial Academy and would then make him secretary of the Moscow area, Krassnaya Priyessnya, which was known to be the most unreliable.

Accordingly, in 1932 Nikita became secretary of the communist cell of the Moscow Industrial Academy, fully realizing that this was a stepping-stone to a brilliant career. Kaganovitch frequently sent for him to attend meetings of the secretaries of cells and districts which were considered important. On these occasions he would speak, and he now accustomed himself more and more to play the part of a "V.I.P." in the workings of the party mechanism.

He was attracting attention. He was being talked about. It had soon become obvious that the young man whom Kaganovitch had taken up was intelligent and wily, with the gift of gab and a close knowledge of all matters relating to "Marxist theory." Further, he had the knack of steering skilfully between the Scylla of the politbureau and the Charybdis of the masses. Above all, he was devoted, heart and soul, to Stalin, the secretary-general of the party.

Nikita never failed to display this devotion in every speech he made, thus following the example of his patron Kaganovitch. While grooming Nikita for his future position, Kaganovitch neglected no opportunity of making him known personally to the men in charge of the party. He began with Molotov, the president of the council, who had been appointed in place of Rykov and who continued for four years as secretary of the central committee, side by side with Stalin.

In a Russian paper published at Bogotá after the last war by a group of émigrés, and entitled *Lutch (The Ray)*, Parkov, a former colonel of the Red Army and at one time officer of Molotov's bodyguard at his country house (he was taken prisoner by the Germans and afterwards declined to be repatriated), mentions the following details:

"As regards Khrushchev, I several times saw him at Molotov's country house in the period between 1931 and 1935. He was always accompanied by Kaganovitch, and they arrived in the car belonging to the secretary of the Moscow party committee. They used to stay for several hours, and sometimes they played bridge."

It will thus be seen that, thanks to Kaganovitch, "Molotov's man," it had become possible for Nikita to be on visiting terms with the president of the council. This was a tremendous success for a newcomer to Moscow, a mere cell-secretary. Kaganovitch introduced him also to Kuibyshev, Orjonikidze, Mikoyan, Kalinin and Kirov. Voroshilov, too, was delighted to extend a welcome to Khrushchev, a veteran of the civil war in the Ukraine.

In 1932 the newspapers announced that Nikita Sergyeyevitch Khrushchev had been appointed secretary of the communist party committee in the Krassnaya Priyessnya district.
In the ordinary way this appointment would have occasioned
no surprise. District secretaries were being replaced every
day, but what aroused comment was the almost solemn manner in which the appointment was formulated. Instead of
being signed by the secretary of the committee of the city of
Moscow, as would normally have been done, Nikita's appointment bore the signature of Joseph Stalin.

A new star had made its appearance on the horizon.

The new secretary of the Krassnaya Priyessnya district
started on his activities by making a clean sweep of the cells
there. Three months before his nomination there had been a
large-scale purge in Moscow. The commission which carried it out, and which was presided over by Kuibyshev, was
ruthless, and nearly twenty-five per cent of the Moscow communists were expelled from the party. In spite of this, Nikita
decided on a purge of his own, and he proved to be even more
severe than Kuibyshev. Acting under his orders, the committee of the party at Krassnaya Priyessnya forwarded to the
GPU a list of those party members who, in accordance with
the decision of the purge-commission, had been expelled.
Nikita reported on the matter to a general district meeting,
and *Pravda* published his report. In it he said:

"The aim of this purge is to track down and expel those
party members who secretly persist in their dastardly opposi-
tional activity against the party and against the Soviet state.
They are traitors, and will be treated as such."

As a result, more than 500 "purged oppositionists" were
handed over to the GPU, and in September 1932 the first
batch of twenty-five "oppositionists" who had been condemned to death entered the Lyubyanka prison. The grim
period of the Big Purge was on its way. Nor was it delayed by

the desperate action of Nadyezhda Aliluyeva, Stalin's wife, who in November 1932 committed suicide in protest against it. Incidentally, this suicide helped Nikita's career. Stalin, who had been on bad terms with his wife for some time, now made no secret of the fact that Rosa, the sister of Kaganovitch, was his mistress, and in the early weeks of 1933 he married her. She was an extremely attractive woman of great intellectual ability (she was a qualified doctor), and she was fond of social life. This caused a change in Stalin's habits, and once a week receptions were held for Stalin's circle of friends at a country house near Moscow. A young Frenchwoman, who was employed as a governess in 1933 for Stalin's children, has given an account of these receptions, an abridgement of which appeared in *The Reader's Digest* in 1949. She did not know the names of the guests, but she refers to a "Ukrainian, secretary of a committee at Moscow" who sometimes attended them. He danced very well, sometimes alone, sometimes with his hostess. He was a good singer and also liked telling anecdotes which made even Stalin laugh. On one occasion, too, he brought with him his little boy[1] who played with Basil, the son of Stalin.

This Ukrainian was obviously Nikita, who at that time was no more than the secretary of the Baumann district, to which he had been transferred after his success at Krassnaya Priyessnya. All the other guests were members of the politbureau or of the Central Council of the communist party. Clearly, Nikita had made headway since he had applied for party membership.

In the Baumann district the conditions were quieter than at Krassnaya Priyessnya. Three purges had already taken place there, and only twenty-eight per cent of the members

---

[1] During the war he served in the air squadron commanded by Basil Stalin, and together with Bulganin's son was killed in 1943 at the Battle of Byelgorod, where Basil Stalin was wounded. Yasha, another of Stalin's sons, was taken prisoner by the Germans and shot by them in 1945.

were left. Nikita was thus able to relax after his strenuous efforts, but Pospyelov, his assistant, did two men's work.

Nikita took advantage of his transfer to the Baumann district to extend his knowledge of Marxism still further. He was often seen at the Karl Marx and Friedrich Engels Institute, where he attended lectures on history and economics. At that time, too, Sokolnikov,[1] a distinguished expert on finance and economics, was delivering lectures on his special subjects, and Nikita attended those as well.

Towards the end of 1934 he was appointed second secretary of the party committee of the city of Moscow. This was a period of dramatic events. On December 1, 1934, Kirov, member of the politbureau, secretary for the Leningrad area and a close friend of Stalin, was assassinated. This had no political significance. It was an act of revenge on the part of one Nikolayev, a young communist, whose wife was Korov's mistress and who had caught the guilty couple together. Stalin, however, enraged and alarmed (Nikolayev was suspected of Trotskyism), decided that the time was ripe for the beginning of a Big Purge, a ruthless slaughter of all the "oppositionists." He was anxious to strike a blow at the "rightists," but he overreached himself. The politbureau, where there was a discussion regarding the desirability of arresting and trying Rykov, Bukharin and Tomsky, was unwilling to endorse Stalin's policy. Kossior, Tchuber, Postychev and Petrovsky, the Ukrainian members of the politbureau, were opposed to Stalin. A number of important Russians, such as Kalinin and Voroshilov, withheld their views. Orjonikidze, the Georgian, the Mikoyan, the Armenian, voted against Stalin's motion. Molotov and Kaganovitch were the only members who supported Stalin wholeheartedly. Stalin adroitly gave in, but he made up his mind to get rid of the

[1] He was the finance commissar who, in 1938, was sentenced to twenty-five years in Siberia, and he died in prison at Yakutsk.

"doubtful elements," that is to say, the opposition members of the politbureau. He suggested to Molotov and Kaganovitch that suitable persons should be earmarked for rapid promotion, so that, in due course, they could supersede the rebels on the politbureau. A list was drawn up, and the names at the head of it were Malenkov, Khrushchev, Yezhov, Beria, Shtcherbatov and Andreyev.

Nikita's career was forging ahead.

VIII

KHRUSHCHEV, MEMBER OF THE POLITBUREAU

In December 1935 Nikita was promoted to first secretary of the party committee of the city of Moscow, and to second secretary of the regional committee, thus becoming the assistant of Kaganovitch. This meant that, in five years he had worked his way upwards from a mere party-cell secretary to the assistant of Kaganovitch, Stalin's brother-in-law, and one of the men who directed the destinies of the immense Soviet Union. His career was not merely rapid, but nothing short of spectacular in a State which had so recently emerged from a revolution, and which was already slipping down an inclined plane towards a bureaucratic hierarchy.

Of all the Soviet notables, Nikita had achieved the most rapid rise towards the peak of power. Circumstances and sheer luck had something to do with it, but he had also geared all his abilities with that object in view. As soon as he became second secretary of the party committee of the city of Moscow, he devoted himself to municipal projects, in which he

had already taken a close interest while secretary of the Krassnaya Priyessnya and Baumann districts. Among these projects, the construction of the underground railway was the
most important. Stalin had decided on this, in spite of the
opposition of Kuibyshev, the president of the Soviet economic council. Kuibyshev had protested against a project
which would entail "squandering" material required for the
vital needs of the country and the people. Stalin had over-
ruled this. He was anxious to make his "reign" memorable by
some large-scale structures, an idea which he had derived
from Alexis Tolstoy's famous novel *Peter the Great*. The
ambitious Georgian, very susceptible to flattery, wanted to
vie with the achievements of Peter. He had already con-
structed a canal from the White Sea to the Baltic. Now he intended to modernize "his" capital city by means of a mag-
nificent underground railway.

Kaganovitch, appointed by the politbureau to supervise
this scheme, was empowered to obtain all the necessary material from the national economic council. Bulganin, president of the Moscow soviet, was appointed director-general of
works, in close co-operation with the technical director, while
Nikita was promoted to be political commissar of the under-
ground-railway scheme. By nominating a political commissar
on this occasion, Stalin sought to emphasize that the under-
taking was of an urgent and almost military character.

The work on the underground railway made very rapid
progress, in spite of the enormous difficulties due to the clayey
soil. Bulganin, the mayor of Moscow, frequently inspected
the works, and as a rule Nikita went with him. The two men
had made a point of establishing a close co-operation between
them. Contrary to the case with other undertakings in Russia, there was never the slightest disagreement between the
director-general and the political commissar during the three
years in which they were working together. An atmosphere of

friendship had developed between them, and they used to meet outside official hours at the country house of one or the other. In 1935 Nikita had been given an elegant little villa for his personal use, about fifteen miles from Moscow, on the road to Ryazan. It had been built by a well-known Soviet architect named Shtchukin, in "old-world" Russian style, with a roof neatly painted red and a weather-vane supported by a cockerel. Nikita had christened his villa "Leleka," which in Ukrainian means "stork". This was perhaps because he recalled the many storks he had seen in the marshes at Kalinovka when he went fishing.

Bulganin had an expert knowledge of alcohol, and he and Nikita soon became boon companions at Leleka Villa, where they spent cozy evenings exchanging confidences. Nikita, although Russified, relished Ukrainian "spotykatch," which was manufactured by the "Beverage Trust" of the Soviet Ukraine in factory No. 5 of the town of Tchiguirin. There was a further special circumstance which greatly helped to cement their friendship. Bulganin has a sister named Nadya, a doctor, who was a close friend of Rosa Kaganovitch. It would appear that Nikita did not remain indifferent to the charms of Nadya, who was ten years his junior.

A Russian historian named Nikolayevsky, a moderate socialist, writing in the *Socialist Courier* (August 1955), a Russian paper published in New York, discussed the part played in the history of Soviet Russia by the "twin souls," Rosa Kaganovitch and Nadya Bulganin. He pointed out the part played by Kaganovitch and his sister at Nizhni-Novgorod in 1918, when Bulganin started his career as assistant to Kaganovitch. He then revealed how the friendship of the two girls, then in their teens, had consolidated the friendship between Kaganovitch and Bulganin, and how Rosa, when she became Stalin's wife, helped Bulganin in his career. The same "twin souls" now helped Nikita.

At the present time we hear a good deal about B. and K., the "terrible twins." This "twinship" is, to a large extent, the handiwork of the "twin souls," Rosa and Nadya. Madam Khrushchev, engrossed in her agricultural research, did not interfere with her husband's friendships. In point of fact, she had become a great friend of Madam Varvara Bulganin, who taught at one of the girls' high schools at Moscow and kept entirely in the background, absorbed by her professional duties. When Nikita with his wife visited Bulganin at his country house, the two ladies spent their time in quiet conversation, while Nikita and Bulganin played tennis singles, or croquet with Nadya and Rosa, if the latter happened to be there.

In 1937 the plenary meeting of the central committee of the Russian communist party, which governed the Soviet Union under the presidency of Stalin, co-opted Nikita as deputy member of the politbureau. That was the year of the Big Purge. Nicholas Ivanovitch Yezhov, the new tycoon of the Tcheka, a sadistic dwarf who made the prisoners of the NKVD, as the GPU was now called, suffer for his bodily affliction, arrested and shot hundreds of members of the communist party, in accordance with the lists drawn up by Stalin personally.

Stalin had an unbounded admiration for Peter the Great and aimed to prove himself his equal. He was familiar with the story of how Peter forced the Russian nobles and ministers to execute with their own hands fifteen hundred of his rebel bodyguard early in the morning on the Red Square. Stalin did not go so far as to force the members of the politbureau themselves to shoot those of his personal enemies whom he had denounced as "lecherous vipers," but he did force them to direct the purges which preceded the executions.

Nikita's first mission was to proceed to the Northern Caucasus, where an extremely severe purge was in progress. He left for Rostov-on-Don by special train, accompanied and escorted by a detachment from the NKVD under Colonel Ivan Serov, now a general, and head of the state security service. In his pocket Nikita had a warrant signed by Stalin. Under the terms of this document, all local authorities were completely at his orders. He had the right to arrest any high official, without referring to the central government of the Soviet Union.

Sheboldayev, the head of the local government, was one of Stalin's relatives, and until 1936 Stalin had trusted him implicitly. He was a regular satrap. In the Kuban region he had enforced the establishment of "kolkhozy," with the result that a civil war had broken out. The Kuban Cossacks had rebelled and advanced towards the towns. Artillery and armored trains had to be sent to check the rebellion. Stalin had congratulated Sheboldayev on having "successfully achieved socialist collectivization." An appalling famine had followed the rebellion. Many of the "kolkhozy" were rendered useless because the peasants had deserted them and decamped towards either the Ukraine or the Volga region. Sheboldayev remained in office and continued to be a member of the central committee of the party. His name had also been submitted for membership of the politbureau.

Suddenly there was a startling revelation. The NKVD of Rostov had discovered some secret correspondence between an "oppositionist" who had been deported to Siberia and Utkin, who was Sheboldayev's personal secretary. When Utkin was arrested and cross-examined he asserted that Sheboldayev knew all about this correspondence and was in secret sympathy with the opposition. In Stalin's eyes this was treason of the most blatant kind: a relative and personal friend who was treating with the enemy. Nikita had therefore been sent to "clarify" the matter. The matter was duly "clarified." Sheboldayev, when arrested and cross-examined, made the fullest possible "confession." He admitted that he was a "saboteur," a fascist agent and a "spy in the pay of Turkey." He confessed that he had deliberately stirred up the rebellion and the famine in the Northern Caucasus to assist in separating the Caucasus from the Soviet Union.

It had taken Nikita only one week to induce a member of the central committee to make all these confessions. On his return to Moscow, by a special decision of the politbureau, he was awarded the Order of Lenin. Sheboldayev, who arrived at Moscow by the same train, was executed in the cellars of the Lyubyanka prison. His execution was not reported in the Soviet press, just as, in the autumn, the execution of Yezhov was also kept secret. For many years Sheboldayev had been praised to the skies in all the newspapers as an "exemplary Stalinist" because of his success in the Northern Caucasus, and it would have been embarrassing to turn him overnight into a "lecherous viper."

Nikita was acknowledged to be more proficient at purges than any other member of the politbureau. His personal situation was invulnerable in that year of grace 1937, when the highest dignitaries of Soviet Russia never knew, when they went to bed, whether or not agents of the NKVD would turn up during the night with a warrant for their arrest, signed by the fearsome Yezhov, or by his deputy Zakovsky, the head of the GPU in the Moscow area. Zakovsky, a former Odessa tough, an "anarchist" at the beginning of the revolution, and a distinguished member of the Tcheka in 1919, was a sadistic scoundrel. He it was who had drawn up a list of traitors, in which he had included, "quite at random," as he admitted on his arrest in August 1938, all the members of the politbureau, except Stalin and Yezhov. Having induced a second-rate prisoner to "confess" that he was "associated" with a prominent functionary on the list of traitors, Zakovsky had the government dignitary arrested immediately. It was as a sequel to the arrest of Yuri Kaganovitch, the brother of Lazar, that

Stalin ordered the arrest of Zakovsky, whose list of traitors was then discovered. Zakovsky was executed, and a month later Yezhov was also arrested and executed.

It is therefore fair to assume that, even if Nikita had been arrested by Zakovsky and had confessed that he was a spy in the service of Poland (this was a confession which all the arrested Ukrainians had to make) on his first cross-examination, Stalin would have saved him, just as he saved Yuri Kaganovitch.

IX

NIKITA IN THE UKRAINE

At the end of 1937 the politbureau had held a special meeting to discuss the situation in the Ukraine. Ever since 1934, when Skrypnik, the old bolshevik and the ring-leader of the "national" Ukrainian communists, committed suicide, a continual series of purges had been carried out in the Soviet Ukraine. Several friends of Skrypnik were arrested and liquidated on December 2, 1934, after the assassination of Kirov. In 1935 about a thousand bolsheviks in the Ukraine were arrested and deported. In 1936 the same fate befell Appolinary Balitzky, the head of the GPU in the Ukraine, and also of about one hundred Ukrainian members of the Tcheka.

Stanislas Kossior, the general secretary of the communist party in the Ukraine, and a deputy member of the politbureau, had been transferred to Moscow. Yezhov had alleged that he was implicated in a "Trotskyist separatist conspiracy," directed by his brother, Vladimir Kossior. The people's council of commissars in the Ukraine was run by Parnas

Lyubtchenko, a former army surgeon, who had very adroitly managed to retain his post.

In December 1937 Stalin launched the Big Purge in the Ukraine. He decided to appoint a general secretary of the central committee of the Ukrainian communist party to ensure complete support by the party while the purge was in progress. For this purpose he needed someone extremely energetic and cunning, capable of carrying on operations skilfully in a region where the national separatist movement was very strong. He first thought of Kaganovitch, who had to his credit his activities as general secretary at Kharkov in 1923 and after, but Kaganovitch demurred. He was unwilling to go to Kiev and become involved needlessly in the blood bath for which his brother-in-law was making preparations. He therefore urged that he should stay at Moscow, and suggested that Nikita should be appointed general secretary of the party at Kiev.

"Comrade Khrushchev is a Ukrainian," he argued. "It would never do to let them say that Ukrainians were being massacred by the 'kazapi'[1] and the 'zhidy.'[2] We must never allow our enemies in the Ukraine to make use of such propaganda as that."

Stalin was persuaded by this argument, and Nikita was sent to Kiev. Nine years after having left the city as a cell-secretary, he was returning there as general secretary of the central committee. All the records relating to rapid careers in the party were broken.

On his arrival Nikita convened a general meeting of the central committee to hear the report of Panas Lyubtchenko, the president of the council. For this purpose, all the "high-ups" of the Ukrainian government, nearly 120 in number, were ordered to attend the plenary committee meeting. When

[1] "Russians" (Ukrainian nickname).
[2] "Jews" (Ukrainian nickname).

they arrived, they discovered that a large-scale police operation was being prepared. The premises of the central committee were surrounded by a detachment of the NKVD forces who had come from Moscow with Nikita. Colonel Serov was in command of them.

The trap was ready and it tricked everyone except Lyubtchenko. When he saw the troops from the NKVD he realized what was afoot. His chauffeur, a Ukrainian communist and an old friend of Lyubtchenko, put his gear in reverse amid the bullets of the Tcheka men. On reaching home, Lyubtchenko barricaded himself, and with the help of his wife, who was also a communist, and his chauffeur, he held out for four hours. When Colonel Serov and his troops forced their way into Lyubtchenko's villa, they found the corpses of Lyubtchenko and his wife, who had blown out their brains with the last of the cartridges.

The plenary meeting of the central committee, presided over by Nikita, ended with a motion deploring the "chauvinistic deviation" of Lyubtchenko and demanding that the guilty men should receive exemplary punishment. This motion was passed unanimously. After the voting, the NKVD detachment came into the chamber. Nikita read out the names from a list which he took from a green dossier. As he read out each name, the respective member was taken into custody there and then, the result being that practically the whole of the Ukrainian government was arrested.

Nikita had done his job with a triumphant flourish, endowing it with all the dash of a *coup d'état*. That day he had tried a new trick and it had worked perfectly. So when, in June 1953, he decided to arrest Beria, he gave a repeat performance.

A week after the death of Lyubtchenko the "party conference," summoned by the new general secretary, endorsed the arrests and executions. Now began a period of hectic activity for Nikita. He carried out purge after purge. He was busily working out a large-scale program of his political schemes.

Meanwhile the Soviet intelligence service was reporting that a European war was drawing near with giant strides. Hitler was getting ready to swallow Austria, after which he would turn his attention to Czechoslovakia. The Ukrainians living in Poland, Czechoslovakia and Rumania were openly talking about the "liberation of the Ukraine from the bolshevik yoke."

The Ukrainian question was of vital importance to the Soviet Union. It was essential to thwart any possible maneuver on the part of Nazi Germany for the purpose of exploiting the Ukraine, "the Piedmont of Russia." After having drawn up his scheme for parrying any such action, he returned to Moscow. He there emphasized to Stalin the necessity for uniting the whole of the Ukraine within the limits of Soviet Russia, in order to "eliminate the danger of seeing the impetus of the Ukrainian national movement turned against Soviet Russia."

In 1947 *Ukrainian Life,* a Ukrainian paper published at Sydney, contained a number of articles by Bormistenko, a former high functionary of the central committee of the communist party at Kiev, and now a refugee. In one of these articles he said:

It must be admitted that Khrushchev's policy was very skilful. He had been responsible for the arrest and execution of Ukrainian Communists, but at the same time he sponsored new editions of Taras Shevtchenko, Franko, Kotsyubinsky and other Ukrainian authors. He spoke Ukrainian with a very unpleasant accent, and he apologized for it whenever he made a speech, but he was very anxious to speak Ukrainian, although he used a few Russian words if he found it necessary to do so. He also used to arrange evening entertainments for the Ukrainian members of the Central Committee. They sang Ukrainian folk-songs and

danced the gopak. Khrushchev joined in these dances. One evening he turned up dressed in the Ukrainian costume of a Cossack, and aroused enormous enthusiasm. When he performed his
dance he was wildly applauded.

This shows that Nikita had not forgotten the dances of his
early years and that he was now turning them to political
account. Bormistenko also mentions the following details:

In May 1939 I accompanied Khrushchev to Moscow. On the
journey he spoke to me at great length, and in the course of his
remarks he expressed the view that it was possible to reach an
agreement with Germany. He went on to say that he had submitted a report to the politbureau, urging that such an agreement should be utilized to create the 'Soviet Greater Ukraine'
and thus settle, once and for all, the problem of Ukrainian ir-
redentism, the arch-enemy of the Soviet Union.

"Germany," he said, "must allow us to add those regions of
Volynia and Podolia, annexed by Poland after the war against
Russia in 1919–20,[1] together with the eastern part of Galicia,
the Carpathian Ukraine,[2] Bessarabia and the Kukovina, which is
also Ukrainian territory. In the opinion of Comrade Potyemkin,[3]
Berlin is prepared to pay a very heavy price for an agreement with
us. We must take advantage of that. It is a historic chance which
will perhaps never again present itself."

Bormistenko later continues:
"Towards the end of our stay at Moscow Khrushchev told
me that this point of view was fully shared by Stalin and
Molotov, who had just been appointed minister of foreign
affairs. Khrushchev rubbed his hands with glee as he said

[1] It was Lenin who, by the Peace of Riga, ceded these areas to Poland. He
feared a new Wrangle offensive in the Crimea. By signing this Peace Treaty
Marshal Pilsudski saved the Soviet State. He made no secret of the fact that
he did so deliberately because he thought that a non-Soviet Russia would not
recognize the Treaty of Riga.

[2] This province was sometimes known also as "Carpathian Russia." In 1918
it was provisionally assigned to Czechoslovakia, but after the war of 1939–45
Dr. Benes ceded it to Soviet Russia.

[3] Deputy-commissar for foreign affairs. He died in 1940 and was succeeded by Vyshinsky.

that he was the one who would achieve something for the Ukraine which would be beyond the power of any other Ukrainian politician or statesman. 'I shall be a Ukrainian Cavour,' he said."

"In August 1939," Bormistenko goes on, "when von Ribbentrop came to Moscow to sign an agreement with Molotov, Khrushchev and I made another journey together to Moscow. Khrushchev had been present at the plenary meeting of the central committee of the communist party summoned by Stalin, who submitted the text of the agreement for ratification. Khrushchev spoke at this meeting and called for an immediate ratification. He stressed the chief advantage of the agreement: Germany promised not to exploit the Ukrainian separatist movement against Soviet Russia, and against the establishment of the 'Soviet Greater Ukraine.' After von Ribbentrop left I was told that Stalin invited Khrushchev and eighteen other members and deputy members of the politbureau to his country house one evening to celebrate the agreement with Nazi Germany. In this connection it is not without interest to quote here certain extracts from the German secret records published in the United States of America. Thus, von Ribbentrop makes the following remarks in his personal papers:

" 'Each time that we discussed with Molotov the question of the Ukrainian territories which were to be re-united with Soviet Russia in accordance with our agreement, Molotov adopted an extremely unyielding attitude. I do not think that this was a personal attitude on his part, as Stalin was just as unyielding as Molotov in matters relating to the Ukrainian territories. I was anxious to obtain more detailed information about this attitude, but our intelligence service could tell me nothing definite. They knew only that there was a Ukrainian among the high Soviet dignitaries, a very influential man, and it was his influence which caused Molotov and

Stalin to adopt their unyielding attitude. I once heard Molotov speak of "our little Ukrainian," in reference to Pavlov, his interpreter, but I do not believe that anyone of that particular caliber could have influenced Stalin or Molotov.'"

The influential Ukrainian mentioned by von Ribbentrop was none other than Nikita Khrushchev. His attitude in the Ukrainian question and his awareness of the danger of a "Ukrainian Piedmont" had greatly impressed Stalin. In 1932 there were several "junior" members of the politbureau, such as Zhdanov, Malenkov and Shtcherbatov, who were outstripping Khrushchev. Zhdanov was already being referred to as Stalin's "Dauphin," and Khrushchev was no match for Zhdanov as regards politics in general. But the Ukrainian question, which he had contrived to transform into a key problem in 1939, on the eve of the Russo-German war, had made him one of the most prominent members of the politbureau.

X

THE PATRIOTIC WAR OF 1941–45

In September 1939 the German-Polish and the Anglo-Franco-German war broke out. For nearly two years Soviet Russia held aloof from the fray. In 1940 the Soviet Ukraine was celebrating its re-unification with those regions of Volynia and Podolia, ceded to Poland under the terms of the Treaty of Riga: Eastern Galicia, Bessarabia and the Bukovina. The Carpathian Ukraine, however, was not detached from Admiral Horthy's Hungary; that was the price paid by Hitler for Hungarian intervention on the side of Germany.

Nikita displayed more energy than ever. He arranged meetings in the re-united territories. He initiated the elections of soviets there. He announced "the great restoration of the Ukrainian Mother Country." Nevertheless, the situation in the Ukraine was far from satisfactory. Bands of partisans were active in the forests there. Trains were often attacked. It became necessary to strengthen security measures and increase the defense forces.

In 1940 Beria, the supreme head of the NKVD, came to
Kiev to acquaint himself with the situation on the spot. He
freely criticized the Ukrainian communist party and the man
at the head of it. This touched off a conflict, the Beria-
Khrushchev conflict. The NKVD report from Kiev was ex-
plicit. If Germany attacked, the majority of the Ukrainian
population would be opposed to Soviet Russia. It would be
impossible to trust the loyalty of the Ukrainian regiments.
In actual fact, when the war with Germany broke out in June
1941, a part of the Ukrainian inhabitants welcomed the German armies. Ukrainian soldiers surrendered in thousands.
It took a whole year before the Ukrainians realized that the
Germans were inflicting upon them a tyranny worse than
that of Stalin.

Khrushchev was appointed president of the defense committee for the Kiev area, with the rank of lieutenant-general.
His task was to assist Marshal Budenny to hold up the Wehrmacht long enough on the right bank of the Dniepr to
enable the Russians to destroy the Dnieprogress dam.
Budenny did not prove accommodating. His popularity and
his personal friendship with Voroshilov and Stalin had made
him high-handed, and he refused to take orders from
Nikita, who in his turn refused to put up with such treatment.
In October 1941 a Tass communiqué announced that
Marshal Budenny had been relieved of his command in the
Ukraine. A week later another communiqué revealed that
a "partisan army" had been formed in the Ukraine. Nikita
was appointed commander-in-chief of this army, with the
rank of colonel-general. But it was his head of staff, Colonel
Syerdyuk, who was in actual command, at his headquarters
in the Briansky forest. Nikita came there by aeroplane every
now and then to carry out a personal inspection and to assist
in the preparations for some surprise attack on the German

rear. As a matter of fact the Germans suffered serious losses in this area, where they were held up for a considerable time. Nikita was twice decorated.

He spent most of his time at the headquarters of Marshal Timoshenko, commander of the southern front, during the extensive preparations which preceded the Kharkov offensive in May 1942. This offensive, which cost the Red Army more than 1,200 armored cars, failed in its purpose, and Kharkov remained in the hands of the Germans. Nevertheless, it was of considerable importance. For two months it held up the German armies and thus prevented them from making an onslaught on Stalingrad. Moreover, it enabled the Russian generals to work out new tactics, which were subsequently employed at Orel, Kursk and Byelgorod. Konyev and quite a number of other military leaders learned their job during this battle in the Ukraine, in which the Russian armored cars did succeed, now and then, in repelling the panzers of the Wehrmacht. It was there that Nikita became a close friend of Konyev, chief of the present supreme general staff and president of the military council of the Soviet high court of justice, which sentenced Beria and others to death in December 1953.

In September 1942, when the danger to Stalingrad became evident, Nikita was seconded as a member of the defense committee ranking immediately after Malenkov, who had been appointed president of this committee. Malenkov did not stay very long at Stalingrad. He was recalled to Moscow to supervise the output of aircraft, of which he had appointed his friend Shakhurov as technical administrator. Nikita, however, remained at Stalingrad. Marshal Zhukov arrived there in September 1942, and Nikita co-operated with him in drawing up the strategic plan of the operations. When Zhukov, in consequence of disagreements with Rokossovsky, commander on the Don front, left Stalingrad (he was replaced by Voronov, general of artillery) Nikita went to Moscow to defend Zhukov against Rokossovsky's accusations. In 1947 Rokossovsky, who had meanwhile been promoted to the rank of marshal (Zhukov was now under a cloud), published his "Memoirs." There he gives his version of what happened, as follows:

We criticized Zhukov for having, by inadvertence, disclosed our strategic plan to the high command of the Wehrmacht. What he did was to appoint at Stalingrad the same sector commanders as during the Battle of Moscow, thus revealing that the plan for the Battle of Stalingrad would be the same as that employed at Moscow.

In October Stalin was not yet jealous of Zhukov. He needed this brilliant strategist, for the war was not nearly over, and the danger was great. Rokossovsky's accusations served merely to delay Zhukov's promotion to the rank of marshal. The fact that Nikita, a representative of the politbureau, had gone to Moscow to defend Zhukov at the politbureau there, brought about a sincere and lasting friendship between him and Zhukov. This incident deserves to be placed on record here. In 1953, after Stalin's death, it was alleged that Zhukov was "Bulganin's man." This is quite untrue. Nikolayev, whom we have already mentioned, has given a detailed account of this matter. He shows that Bulganin, appointed commissar at the first front in White Russia in 1944, which was under Zhukov's command, had been on very indifferent terms with Marshal Zhukov, and of his own accord had asked to be transferred to the second front in White Russia, under the command of Rokossovsky, the opponent of Zhukov. We also know that Nikita, appointed commissar of the politbureau on the first Ukrainian front, under the command of Konyev, had combined these functions with those of commissar to Zhukov.

He was one of the men who defended Zhukov at the polit-bureau whenever Zhukov needed such defense, and he needed it very often, for he was frequently at odds with the political commissars of the armed forces.

It was owing to Nikita's support that Zhukov had succeeded in having the political commissars removed, except for the politbureau commissars with the commanders of a battle front. It is also worth noting that in March 1955, when after the resignation of Malenkov, he was appointed minister of war, he again demanded that the corps of political commissars should be abolished. Quite recently, too, on the eve of the twentieth party congress, he repeated this demand.

Meanwhile, the war was still in progress. The victory at Stalingrad marked the decisive turning point, the beginning of the end of the Wehrmacht. But the enemy was not yet defeated. In February 1943 the Germans had recaptured Kharkov. Nikita was sent to the Voronezh area, where the "first army of the steppes" was formed, under the command of Marshal Konyev.

Kissilev, a Soviet journalist, who visited Konyev's head-quarters "somewhere north-east of Kursk," gave a graphic account of his visit in a book entitled *The Military Achievement* and published at Moscow in 1947. He says:

Marshal Konyev, commander-in-chief of the army of the steppes, was at his headquarters at X. I entered a large room, decorated with a portrait of Comrade Stalin. On a table covered with a pink cloth a map of the Kursk-Voronezh area was spread out.

The Marshal was examining the map. By his side there was another comrade who had evidently just told him something funny. The commander-in-chief of the army of the steppes was laughing heartily.

On seeing me enter, he said:

"Ah, it's you, Kissilev. Glad to see you. I remember you from the conference at the central military and naval club in Moscow!"

Then, turning to the man beside him, he said:

"Nikita Sergyeyevitch, allow me to introduce you to Comrade Kissilev, the eye of military public opinion."

I then recognized Comrade Khrushchev, whom I had seen at the same club. He shook hands with me very affably and said:

"So you're an eye, are you? That's all right, provided you don't squint."

He laughed at his own joke and added:

"You have a keen scent. The scent of a greyhound of the press. Well, you're going to be given a scoop."

He broke off, eyed the Marshal and said:

"What do you think, Vanya? Should we tell him the news?"

The Marshal nodded.

"Very well then. Now listen to me, young man. The army of the steppes is a thing of the past. From today onwards we are the first Ukrainian front. You can let your paper know that, although officially it won't be announced until next week. But don't give me away to Comrade Shtcherbatov.[1] I'm scared of him. He's a holy terror and he might send me to——"

He added a very racy expression, to the delight of Marshal Konyev, who roared with laughter.

Comrade Khrushchev then went to a small cupboard, opened it and took out a decanter containing a red beverage. He said:

"We aren't allowed to drink alcohol. But in honor of the first Ukrainian front we're going to drink some vishnyovka."[2]

He poured out a glass of it for me.

"Long live the first Ukrainian front! Long live Nikita Khrushchev! Long live Marshal Konyev!" I exclaimed.

Nikita remained in the army until the Ukraine had been completely cleared of German troops. He then went back to Kiev to attend to the reconstruction of the region. There had been wholesale destruction, and ruined buildings were to be seen on all sides. A great part of the population had been deported to labor camps in Germany. The peasantry, accus-

---

[1] Member of the politbureau and head of the censorship during the war. He died in 1944.

[2] Ukrainian cherry brandy.

tomed to an existence without the "Kolkhozy,"[1] had, for all practical purposes, shared out the land and were tilling it individually. Rapid reconstruction was not possible, because more than 3,000,000 Ukrainians had been deported by the NKVD for "collaboration with the Germans."

Nikita was shrewd enough not to return to the Ukraine until after the purges carried out by the agents of the NKVD, at the direct orders of Beria. With his inborn flair he guessed that the day would come when it would be possible to saddle Beria with deporting no less than 3,000,000 Ukrainians to Siberia for the sole crime of "breathing the same air as the invaders."[2] But in 1945–47 he was not yet "liberal." He was introducing stern measures for the purpose of "retrieving the material resources of the 'kolkhozy' which had been looted by the criminals," and by "criminals" he here meant the peasants.

In 1948 he asked Stalin to relieve him, for one year, of his functions as general secretary of the Ukrainian communist party, and to appoint him head of the government in the Ukraine. He had a scheme of his own for making the peasants return to the bosom of "integral socialism." Melnik, one of Nikita's men, took his place as general secretary. Nikita himself began to put his scheme into operation. It involved the construction of garden cities, elimination of backward villages, the electrification of agriculture, the "centralization of the kolkhozy."

---

[1] At the beginning of the occupation, the Germans had retained the "kolkhozy" or collective farms. Hitler was of the opinion that Nazi Germany should take advantage of "this clever arrangement introduced by the communists for the purpose of exploiting the peasantry," as it was described by Alfred Rosenberg, high commissioner for Eastern Europe. In 1945, when defeat was close at hand, the "kolkhozy" were broken up.

[2] This is a quotation from a play written by Korniyeytchuk, a Ukrainian dramatist, of whom Nikita was a patron. The play exposes "the cruelties of Beria's NKVD." It was very successful in the Ukraine in 1955.

The "kolkhoz" peasant was to become a wage-earner like his city comrade working in industry. No more small holdings.[1] Such was the basis of Nikita's new scheme.

[1] The "kolkhozy" peasants are entitled to small holdings, ranging in area from about half an acre to one acre, where they can cultivate a kitchen garden, an orchard, etc., and also grow food for the two cows, the small cattle and the poultry to which they are entitled.

XI

NIKITA, SECOND SECRETARY OF THE CENTRAL PARTY COMMITTEE

The year 1949 was checkered with crises and squabbles in Stalin's immediate set. The atmosphere of deep secrecy which prevailed at Moscow prevented foreign observers from discovering the underlying reasons for these crises, although there were certain events which provided a partial explanation.

The first of these events was a plenary meeting of the central committee which dealt with the report of Andreyev, secretary of the committee and member of the politbureau. The subject of the report was agriculture.

The "kolkhozy" were proving very unsatisfactory. The peasants preferred to work on their small holdings, and Mukhin, an instructor in the agricultural section of the central committee, had shown that the "kolkhoz" peasants exerted themselves as much in a single day's labor on their individual allotments as during a whole week's work in the "fields of the socialist sector."

Andreyev had introduced a system of his own, by which

the "kolkhoz" peasants worked in teams, called "brigades," under a "brigadier" who was a member of the communist party. This "militarism" of work made it possible to tighten up supervision. The "brigadier" had authority to order the arrest of those who worked badly, but the results continued to be poor. The peasants did their work on the ca' canny principle.

Andreyev was severely criticized and dismissed from his post. Circular No. 77, issued on February 28, 1948, by the central committee, ordered the reorganization of the brigades under the management of Benediktov, a communist agrarian and a member of the central committee. But the reorganization was very slow in producing the expected results.

In the sphere of foreign policy Stalin had met with a tremendous setback: Tito's defection, Zhdanov, the second secretary of the central committee, who was responsible for relations with foreign communist parties, had fallen into disfavor and died of a stroke shortly afterwards. Voznessensky, president of the state planning department and a member of the politbureau, was accused of "economic defeatism," for refusing to believe in the possibility of the automatic collapse of capitalism as a sequel to a world-wide economic crisis. He was removed from office and deported to Siberia, where he was executed on Stalin's orders.

The cold war and the Berlin blockade were creating the danger of a new world-war, and the whole situation forced Stalin to reorganize the secretariat of the central committee as a means for tackling this new set of difficulties. He now remembered the "Ukrainian prodigy" Nikita Khrushchev, that all-rounder, who could not only dance, sing and tell funny stories in his country villa, but was also a live wire and an expert organizer. In the scheme for the new secretariat of the central committee, Nikita was to occupy a foremost position.

Stalin, the general secretary, reserved for himself the task of "general supervision," but in actual practice the central committee was directed by the first secretary, George Malenkov, a comparatively young man (he was born in 1902) a dignitary of the party and whole-heartedly devoted to Stalin. He was, in fact, his henchman and personal agent.

Nikita, the second secretary, was to direct the agricultural and industrial sections of the central committee. In case of an "economic setback" he would have had to shoulder the entire responsibility. Then there was Susslov, the third secretary, who had to deal with the press, propaganda and the "fraternal parties" (this meant the foreign communist parties), under Malenkov's guidance. Pospyelov, secretary of the Moscow regional committee, became the fourth secretary of the central committee, with Ponomarenko, former secretary of the White Russia committee, as fifth secretary. Finally, Andreyanov (secretary at Leningrad), Ignatov and Ignatyev were to be the fifth, sixth and seventh secretaries respectively.

In this way the dictator's personal cabinet was to be set up. Stalin did not intend to submit any longer to the formality of cooperative leadership in the politbureau, or at meetings under the auspices of the president of the council. He had made up his mind to deal with everything in his own bureau, and the reformed secretariat would enable him to do this. Its activities started in 1949.

Nikita set the ball rolling with a large-scale plan for the reorganization of the "kolkhozy." He expressed the view that the "brigadier" system was merely a "petty-bourgeois deviation," and that the structure of the "kolkhozy" would have to be fundamentally changed. According to him, it was necessary to bring about a "wholesale reduction of the 'kolkhozy,'" just as he had already done in the Ukraine, to build "garden cities" for the peasants. Their huts in the villages were to be pulled down, and they were to be transferred, by force, if necessary, to "thoroughly up-to-date buildings in the garden cities," where "the petty-bourgeois mentality would be quickly transformed into the mentality of wage-earning workers in a socialist state." The fields were to be "electrified," and electric power would make it possible to operate "trolley-bus tractors" upon them. This would kill two birds with one stone: the peasants would be transformed into "agricultural proletarians," and it would be possible to economize in the use of gasoline for the tractors, gasoline being essential for the national defense.

Nikita's imagination now ran away with him. He made excited speeches in which he gave details of life in the "future city of socialism attaining triumphant agricultural successes." But he not only talked; he acted as well. While Stalin, Molotov, Voroshilov, Malenkov and Kaganovitch were arguing about foreign policy and acting as hosts to Mao-Tse-Tung, who came to Soviet Russia in the autumn of 1949 and stayed there until March 1950 when he signed his agreements, Nikita was "organizing the garden cities."

He started with the Moscow region, in which some 7,000 "kolkhozy" had been reduced to 1,200. More than 500 villages were demolished and their inhabitants transferred to the "up-to-date City of victorious socialism." This "up-to-date City" consisted merely of a long row of hutments which bore an odd resemblance to a concentration camp, except that there was no barbed wire. The peasants, before voting in favor of a "voluntary transfer" to the "up-to-date City," sold their cattle, or slaughtered it under the pretext that they were going to "celebrate the disappearance of the last traces of capitalism in agriculture."

When in the autumn of 1955 Nikita delivered his speech on the shortage of meat and the decrease of livestock in the Soviet Union, he omitted to point out that one of the many reasons for this falling-off was the transfer of the peasants to the "garden cities." Though busy with the reorganization of agriculture, Nikita had not forgotten industry. Bulganin, a new member of the politbureau, was responsible for this particular matter. Thus, the old friends had come together again, and they quickly established a close co-operation.

Soviet industry was directed by the technician party members, the majority of whom were former students of the Moscow College of Technology, where Malenkov had been trained. This made it possible for him to exercise a marked ascendancy over the "technocratic bureaucrats." This, together with his influence with the provincial party committees, caused him to be regarded as a leading figure by a large section of the bureaucrats who direct the national economy of the huge trust known as the Soviet Union.

Bulganin, who had become a marshal and minister of war, had the most expert knowledge of economic and financial questions. He was one of Stalin's trusted advisers and had been instructed by him to supervise the activities of certain branches of heavy industry. Nikita and Bulganin had agreed that this "supervision" should fall heavily upon the friends of Malenkov. The historian Nikolayevshy describes how an inspection by Bulganin very adversely affected Shakhurin, the minister of aircraft construction, who was a close friend of Malenkov. He was dismissed and sent to the Vorkuta concentration camp. Nikita took advantage of this to try and strike a blow at Malenkov's influence with Stalin.

Nikita played an important part also in the rehabilitation of Marshal Zhukov, who had been exiled to Sverdlovsk. He argued that, in view of the international tension, it was necessary to have an outstanding strategist at the head of the army, and he therefore urged that Zhukov should be brought back to Moscow to be appointed head of the general staff and in close touch with the minister of war. Bulganin concurred.

Stalin agreed to Nikita's suggestion, in spite of strong opposition by Malenkov, who favored Marshal Vassilevsky. On his return from exile, Zhukov was appointed vice-minister of war. Rokossovsky, his personal enemy, was packed off to Poland and transformed into the "first Polish marshal."

In May 1952 Nikita and Stalin paid a visit to the "garden cities" in the Moscow region. In those which they inspected they saw dwellings equipped with all modern comfort, paved streets, and aerials for wireless and television installed on the house tops. There were popular rejoicings and dancing in the streets to welcome the two distinguished guests. Children offered flowers to "Grandfather" Stalin, while Nikita remembered the days of his youth at Kalinovka, and, borrowing an accordion, played Ukrainian folk tunes and danced with the girls and young women, to the amusement and amazement of Stalin.

History repeats itself. In 1822, just 130 years before this, Tsar Alexander II, accompanied by General Araktcheyev, his "Khrushchev," had visited the "garden cities" of the peasant colonists in the region of Novgorod. General Araktcheyev, who was of peasant origin, danced with the colonists, to the Tsar's keen enjoyment.

Nikita was awarded a decoration, and this made the sixteenth which he had received.

In June 1952 Stalin had begun to make preparations for the nineteenth pan-Russian congress of the communist party. He had made up his mind to abolish the politbureau, the last relic of Leninist co-operation between colleagues. Nikita was instructed to draw up a draft of the new party statutes. This was a mark of Stalin's implicit confidence, for Nikita, who in 1917 had not yet been a member of the party, was now entrusted with a task of the utmost importance. The reform was a far-reaching one. Not only was the politbureau to be done away with, but Stalin had also decided to drop the word "bolshevik" from the name of the party, which henceforward was to be called "The communist party of the Soviet Union", instead of the "Pan-Russian bolshevik communist party." The "bolsheviks" were the men who had struggled side by side with Lenin against Tsarism. Lenin himself, Zinovyev, Kamenev, Krestinsky, Bukharin, Rykov, Tomsky and hundreds of others had been the "old bolsheviks." All of them except Lenin had been shot in the cellars of the NKVD. The continuity between the old and the new party, the statutes of which were drafted by Nikita, was now represented by Stalin alone. He was the only bolshevik left of the "old guard." But he never wanted to hear the word bolshevik again. He wanted to get rid of the old statute which had been drawn up by those whom he had ruthlessly executed, after stigmatizing them as "lecherous vipers."

In that year, 1952, Stalin may have been pondering upon a scheme for a gigantic conflict, a huge, world-wide holocaust, in which China, now communist, would be his stand-by. He may not have intended that this, the final, struggle should be waged under the bolshevik standard of Lenin, for if he gained the victory, the others, his victims, would also gain honor when the history of their times came to be written. Perhaps, too, the Moscow trials would then be investigated, and the forgeries prepared by Jezhov and Vyshinsky at Stalin's orders would be detected. That may have been why Stalin wished to go down in history under his own standard: the communist party of the Soviet Union, Stalin's party.

He selected Nikita, then, to draw up the new party statutes. In his eyes, Nikita was a tractable functionary, a "newcomer" who would discard the name of bolshevik without the slightest difficulty. But in selecting Nikita for this task he took a step the significance of which he could not foresee. He made Nikita the fugleman of the party bureaucrats who were to govern Russia after Stalin was no more.

XII

THE DEATH OF STALIN

In October 1952 the nineteenth pan-Russian congress of the bolshevik-communist party was held at Moscow. A sinister and stifling atmosphere prevailed there. The members of the politbureau realized that the general secretary was about to spring a maneuver upon them which would very seriously affect the home and foreign policy of the Soviet Union.

Stalin refrained from reading to the congress the political report of the central committee. This was the first time he had acted in this manner, and his silence boded nothing but menace. The report was read by Malenkov. Nikita submitted a report on the organization of the cadres and the new party statutes.

Molotov, in one of his usual drab speeches, merely touched upon the subject of foreign policy.

Malenkov's delivery was monotonous. He spoke with an Orenburg accent, and he came out with sentences, the structure of which infringed the rules of Russian syntax.

Nikita spoke in his customary spirited manner, and his

slight Ukrainian accent rather beguiled his audience. He sprinkled his speech with proverbs, illustrative parallels, anecdotes. The members of the congress were induced to forget that the point at issue was the destruction of the historical bolshevik party, and laughed heartily at the anecdotes and proverbs, many of which had been made up by Nikita on the spur of the moment.

Then came the debate on the new statutes. Strictly speaking, there was no real debate. The hard-bitten members of the politbureau, beginning with Mikoyan, expressed their "profound admiration for the great architect of socialism, Stalin, the prodigious comrade, the leader of progressive humanity." The provincial representatives went even further than this. A deputy from Azerbaidjan read a poem of his own manufacture, in which Stalin was extolled in the oriental manner, the same terms being used as those in which the sultans and the shahs had been extolled in the past.

When the "debate" was over, Nikita read out the list of members of the new central committee, as proposed by Stalin. The list was unanimously adopted by acclamation, instead of being put to a secret vote in accordance with the party statutes.

On the following day the papers published the list of members of the presidium of the central committee, which superseded the politbureau, and the list of members of the secretariat. No further doubt was possible. Stalin was hatching some maneuver with a bearing upon both home and foreign policy, and of a scope which could not yet be conjectured. He had introduced into the presidium, which had twenty-five members and eleven deputy members, quite a number of insignificant persons, mere supers. The secretariat had been distended. It now comprised: Stalin, general secretary; Malenkov, first secretary; Khrushchev, second secretary; Ponomarenko, third secretary; Susslov, fourth secretary;

Ignatyev, fifth secretary; Aristov, sixth secretary, and Breynev, Pyegov, Mikhailov and Ignatov, who were also secretaries but were not numbered. It was obvious that Stalin intended to turn his secretariat into a kind of "Ersatz consultative politbureau."

In November 1952 the situation became critical. Ignatyev,
the fifth secretary, was appointed head of the political secret
police, just as in 1936 Stalin had appointed Yezhov, the fifth
secretary of the central committee, head of the NKVD on the
eve of the Big Purge. It looked as though Stalin was no longer
making any secret of his intentions. His object was to terrify
everyone by conjuring up the specter of a new Big Purge.

In December the first batch, the "murderers in white overalls," were arrested. These were the doctors of the Kremlin
polyclinic, eighty per cent of them being Jews. The dignitaries of the régime knew the names on the list before they
were disclosed by "Tass." Stalin's plan was now quite evident.
There was to be another grim purge, perhaps even more
ghastly than the previous one carried out under the auspices
of Yezhov. The proceedings against the doctors were conducted with an altogether novel speed, wholly unlike the
slow techniques employed for securing spontaneous confessions.

Ryumin, head of the investigation department of the secret police, was now adopting the techniques of the Gestapo.[1]
His concern was to strike and to strike quickly, with the object
of clearing the ground for the start of the Big Purge, which
was to take place between the spring and summer of 1953.
Such was certainly the political directive which Stalin supplied to Ignatyev and Ryumin. The former, whose time was
taken up with his activities on the central committee, where

[1] Of the sixteen persons arrested in December 1942, eleven were not liber-
ated until March 1953, while five of them had died as the result of their treatment during the enquiries.

he had still remained, left it to Ryumin to determine when the operation was to start. Ryumin decided that this could best be done by exploiting his denunciation of Madam Timutchuk, a doctor attached to the Kremlin polyclinic. The secret police in the Soviet Union enjoyed a considerable degree of independence. The nature of their activities ruled out any permanent and effective supervision, quite apart from the fact that most of the members of the politbureau preferred to wash their hands of everything and endorse convictions in accordance with "confessions made in the presence of the attorney-general of the Soviet Union," Vyshinsky, Rudenko, Gontcharov and others.

Ryumin did not take action at random. The "anti-Zionist" denunciations of Madam Timutchuk had, doubtless, not reached his office by mere chance. General Poskrebytchev, the head of Stalin's private secretariat and his evil genius, could have informed him about a quarrel between Stalin and his wife, Rosa Kaganovitch, and Stalin's intention to marry a lady from far up the Volga. But the beginning of the purge was badly timed. The accusation of "Zionism in the service of American imperialism" was bound to lead, sooner or later, to a charge against Kaganovitch, who had been in close touch with Molotov. He it was, too, who favored the rise of Malenkov, and who, in 1918, had become an associate of Bulganin. He was, too, as we have already seen, on intimate terms with Nikita as well. He had instigated the appointment of many red directors of industry in the Soviet Union. Finally, he was the head of a brain trust, established at Stalin's orders, to cope with the setbacks in the economic activities, in the industries, finances and transport system of the Soviet Union.

Panic spread like wildfire in Moscow, and indeed throughout the Soviet Union, among the upper crust of the bureaucrats. Even Beria, though outside the Kaganovitch clique, was not immune—his mother was a Jewess. Nikita, too, who had recently been promoted to second secretary of the central committee, must have felt considerable qualms.

What exactly was Stalin aiming at? Did he want to maintain the threat of a military conflict as a means for achieving by bloodshed "debourgeoisation" of Soviet Russia? Or was it his intention to achieve this process by actually unleashing a military conflict? In our opinion, the latter was his real aim. But neither Stalin nor Poskrebytchev, his henchman, is available to answer these questions. It will be easier to find an answer to them by considering the exact situation of the Soviet Union in February 1953, on the eve of Stalin's death.

The practical application of "socialism in a single country" and of state capitalism (the communist party holding a monopoly of the available power for a world-wide expansion of his ideas and system of government) had brought Stalin's Soviet Union into existence. Its main feature was a bureaucratic hypertrophy unprecedented in human records. Out of the 55,000,000 state employees, there were 45,000,000 manual workers and 10,000,000 bureaucrats, 1,000,000 of whom operated the party mechanism (the "apparatchiki"). This element, which, from the point of view of the national economy, was purely parasitic, controlled the 18,000,000 communist party members and young communists (the present number is 25,000,000), the only organized power in the Soviet Union.

Stalin had granted the bureaucracy in the Soviet Union the right to own, as their private property, villas, cars and unlimited banking accounts, as well as racing stables. They were allowed the use of servants, who were designated as "assistant workers in the home." They had received the privilege of bequeathing their property without paying any succession duty, which, although heavy in the Soviet Union, is less so than in the United States of America, to say nothing of Great Britain.

The bureaucrats had now become the backbone of the régime. More and more they realized how great was the power derived from their personal property, which was constantly on the increase. They had achieved and consolidated a prosperity recently acquired by brute force. The result was that they were beginning to lose their revolutionary ardor and their willingness to sacrifice their gains in the interests of the world-wide revolution, which was the ultimate aim of Stalin and of his "church of militant Marxism."

It was clear that, if a new world-wide conflict were to break out, the Soviet bureaucrats would take advantage of it to try and seize control of the government. This would not be difficult, because they numbered 10,000,000, of whom at least 5,000,000 were communists, apart from the 1,000,000 communists who were "apparatchiki." Thus, the danger was no longer outside the party, as it had been during the civil war of 1918–20, but within the party. That is why Stalin may have determined to smash the "bureaucratic backbone" of the Soviet Union, and he had to begin with the communist bureaucrats, as well as their friends in the central committee of the party and the former politbureau. After having played the parts of Danton, Marat, Robespierre, Barras and even of a victorious Napoleon, Generalissimo Stalin apparently intended to make ready for a final conflict, in the manner of Baboeuf, as a leader of the "equals" against the privileged men whom he himself had fashioned. This time he was acting the sorcerer's apprentice by pitting himself against a force which his own state socialism had created and which was almost invincible. He could smash this force only by smashing his own State, by interfering with the historical continuity of Russia, by shattering that vast structure which had been salvaged and extended as a result of his victory over Hitler.

A quirk of fate had brought Stalin into history at a juncture, when Russia vitally needed someone to come forward who could salvage her territories. As long as Stalin kept to the scenario demanded by the logic of history, he continued to be "great" and "prodigious," in spite of his intellectual short-comings, his cruelty, his treacherous nature and his appalling lack of any moral standards. But as soon as he sought to tamper with the scenario, he was bound to come to grief—just like the victims of his purges, to whom Russian national interests were of no account as compared with some hair-splitting ideology swallowed holus-bolus in the Marxist kitchen.

Tolstoy brought out this principle very clearly when he said:

The men called "great" are entitled to this epithet only as long as they limit themselves to directing the course of events which destiny has set in motion in their historical period. The instant that they rebel, the instant that they seek to resist what is historically inevitable, a single step leads them from the sublime to the ridiculous, and they go to their destruction.

Why did Stalin resist the destiny which had marked him out as the founder of a new Russian State? Why did he seek to revert to the conditions prevailing in the period which had long been swept away by the revolution?

During his stay in Belgrade Nikita, elevated by Marshal Tito's shlivovitza, applied the answer:

It was one of those cases of a reversion to the sustenance of the past, such as happens to men in the evening of their days when pure reason begins to be shrouded by the shadows of the past.

Stalin had started his career as an egalitarian revolutionary. In an interview with Emil Ludwig, he had said quite sincerely:

I became a revolutionary in my youth because I wanted to establish liberty and equality in place of oppression.

He had established a tyranny such as the world had never before seen, except in Hitler's Germany. And he was not fated to die until the day when he decided to revert to the ideas of his early days in Georgia and to become a "revolutionary mountaineer," to fight against the State which he had created, to shatter the historical continuity of Russia. He vanished from the scene and left his place vacant. Another was to occupy his chair of office in the presidium of the central committee.

That other was Nikita Sergyeyevitch Khrushchev.

XIII

THE STRUGGLE FOR STALIN'S SUCCESSION—I

The generalissimo's sudden illness aroused a panic throughout Russia. The servile press had so accustomed people to regarding Stalin as synonymous with the State, as the "invincible and infallible chief", as "the mighty leader" and so forth, that the news of his illness caused everyone to share the same misgivings: when Stalin is taken from us, our enemies will undoubtedly attempt to invade our country, and they could hardly choose a moment more favorable for them.

When Stalin did die, the presidium kept his death a secret for four whole days, and the alarm among its members asserted itself more and more. The "apparatchiki," the most influential section of Soviet bureaucracy, were anxious to emphasize their preponderance by nominating a new general secretary of the party. The bureaucrats in the departments dealing with industry, finance and transport likewise wished to have a representative of theirs at the helm. In an economy based on state capitalism they were the most powerful section of the new privileged class, but they lacked a "Russian" candidate, their candidates, Mikoyan and Kaganovitch, being "foreigners."

The military men had no candidate among the party "high-ups." Although Zhukov had joined the party in 1919, he was still a very retiring member of the communist hierarchy even in 1953. Voroshilov, again, was no longer taken into account as a possible candidate by the military caste. The deplorable part he had played in 1937, during the sinister purge which had drained the blood of the Red Army, had discredited him once and for all. Marshal Bulganin, though minister of war in 1953, was not one of the military candidates, either. As former president both of the state bank and the federative republic of Russia, he was more of a financial bureaucrat than a member of the military caste.

Molotov, the former right-hand man of Stalin, completely lacked popularity among the people and in the party. The nickname "kamenny zad" (stone backside), which Bukharin had bestowed upon him, stuck to him for the rest of his life. Finally, Beria, the representative of the secret police, was universally detested, and was a Georgian into the bargain.

The newly elected presidium of the central committee consisted of ten members and two deputy members: Malenkov, Khrushchev, Beria, Bulganin, Molotov, Kaganovitch, Mikoyan, Voroshilov, Saburov, Susslov, Pervukhin and Ponomarenko. It took the presidium two days to decide upon the succession. To begin with, the principle of co-operative leadership was proclaimed. This meant that there would be no general secretary of the party, and not even a first secretary of the central committee. Next came the announcement that the president of the council would be "assisted" by several "first deputies," without whose agreement no decision could be reached. It was also decided to "decapitate" the secretariat of the central committee by appointing Malenkov president of the council.

The first council of ministers was merely the outcome of a compromise between the various sections of the soviet bureaucracy. Nikita was relegated to the rank of "secretary of the central committee," and thus became a comparative underling—seventh or eighth among the dwellers on the post-Stalin Olympus. But he quickly contrived to take his revenge.

At the beginning of April 1953 Malenkov started on a long tour of the Soviet Union, and Nikita accompanied him. They visited the Ukraine, the Northern Caucasus, the Volga area, the Urals. Wherever they went, it was Nikita who did the talking. He proclaimed the beginning of a new era, "the era of co-operation between colleagues." In this way he posed as one who favored the removal of local tyrants, whose numbers had greatly increased during the Stalin era. The people in the provincial districts could, in a pinch, put up with the tyranny of a "central headman," distant and unseen, but they strongly resented a local jack-in-office who, only a day or two previously, had been one of themselves, and who was now behaving like a satrap. Nikita's reputation as a "protector against the tyranny of local satraps" spread like wildfire. Hitherto almost unknown in the Urals, on the Volga, and in the Caucasus, he was now blossoming forth as a "friend of the people," a personality whom everyone knew and liked. His abilities as an orator, his brogue, his proverbs and his funny stories added rapidly to his popularity.

While Malenkov was sending audiences to sleep with his speeches, Nikita strolled about in the corridors, talked as man to man with everyone he met there, answered the most ticklish questions with the utmost frankness, and listened to grievances.

On his return to Moscow, Nikita found Bulganin at loggerheads with Beria. Bulganin had for the time being retained his position as president of the council, and this had inflamed Beria's fierce animosity. To make matters worse, Bulganin, acting in his joint capacity as minister of war and president of the council, had signed and issued an order that, henceforward, the Moscow MVD troops were to come within the jurisdiction of the military authority of the Moscow area, and not that of the ministry of the interior. The commander of the area, Colonel General Moskalenko, visited all the barracks and personally read out Bulganin's order.

After the death of Stalin, Beria tried to act the part of a "big shot." He also sought to curry favor with the people. After the rehabilitation of the "murderers in white overalls," he went so far as to proclaim an amnesty for petty criminals and to abolish the camps at Magadan and Vorkuta, where some 500,000 internees had been held. He even sent his "emissaries" abroad to "sound" Western intentions, quite independently of the ministry of foreign affairs. He appointed the heads of the MVD without consulting the presidium of the central committee. Beria was by no means a conspirator, but all his actions justified his enemies in describing him as such. Thus, he corresponded with his underlings in the provincial areas, especially with Dekanozov, head of the MVD in the Caucasus, by means of a personal code. During his trial in December 1953 his letters were read in court. They had been deciphered in a special section of the central committee, under Nikita's auspices. It has been stated that Beria protested against the deciphering process, on the ground that it had distorted the meaning of the letters.

In May 1953 Beria was at the end of his tether. Moskalenko was in command of the MVD troops in Moscow. General Serov had been appointed head of the Moscow regional section of the MVD. But instead of adopting a pliant attitude, as he had done while Stalin was still alive, Beria persisted in his "opposition" policy. He wrote a letter to his friend Lomanidze in Tiflis full of insults and threats against Bulganin and Khrushchev, whom he described as "villainous accomplices." He suggested that a special board should be set up to organize an extraordinary congress of the communist party. He proceeded to the Soviet zone in Germany, where he transmitted to General Gretchko instructions for the maintenance of order and security in Eastern Berlin. These instructions prevented the slaughter of the people in Berlin by Russian armored cars in June 1953. Beria had not submitted his instructions to the presidium of the central committee for approval. The die was now cast.

On June 25, 1953, Nikita called a conference in his office at the central committtee. Bulganin, Mikoyan, Voroshilov, Kaganovitch, Saburov, Pervukhin and Susslov were present on this occasion. Thus, including Nikita, eight members of the presidium, a majority, attended this meeting. Nikita had fought shy of bringing up for debate by the presidium in a body the topic with which he dealt at this conference, and which, in fact was nothing less than the arrest of Beria, himself a member of the presidium.

Towards the end of the conference, Marshals Zhukov and Konyev, General Moskalenko and General Serov, head of the MVD in the Moscow area, arrived. Marshal Voroshilov, in his capacity as president of the supreme soviet, had by now signed a warrant for the arrest of Beria and his accomplices. The two generals were instructed to execute the warrant. Although Nikita had taken the precaution of bolstering himself with a majority of the presidium, the arrest of Beria looked more like a pronunciamento than a legal act. Nikita had established a precedent.

But he had reason to consider that this precedent involved no danger to himself. Beria was a "vyskotchka," an upstart with a dubious past. He was the master of the MVD which was detested by bureaucrats, masses and military circles alike. It was easy for Nikita to camouflage his "settlement of accounts" with Beria as a measure for "liberalizing" the régime, and to make it the starting point for this "liberalizing" process. He was eliminating an enemy, and at the same time gaining tremendous political capital at home and abroad.

The presidium and a plenary meeting of the central committee expressed approval of Beria's arrest. It was also decided to expel him from the communist party and to declare his cupability under the terms of the law of December 1, 1934, which had been promulgated on the day of the assassination of Kirov. Marshal Konyev and Rudenko, the provost marshal who took part in the Nuremberg trials, were instructed to deal with the Beria case.

After having agreed to the arrest of Beria, his colleagues washed their hands of the whole business, and left it to the military authorities to take all necessary action. The MVD, as far as its connections with the secret political police were concerned, was abolished and replaced by the state security committee, directed by General Serov.

No sooner was Beria eliminated than Nikita plunged into a feverish activity. He made speeches. He delivered lectures. Most of them dealt with the food situation in the Soviet Union. Under Stalin's dictatorship very little thought had been given to this subject. It was frequently talked about, the conclusion always being that "everything was making satisfactory progress", that "the Soviet Union had far more cereals, meat and other forms of nutriment" than before the revolution, and so on. Nobody explained why it was that the workers had only a remote chance of an increase of their daily rations, but this aspect of the matter counted for little during the Stalin period.

Nikita's object was to "come down to brass tacks" with the masses. In one of his sensational talks he informed his bewildered audience that "Soviet Russia had fewer cattle than there had been in tsarist Russia," and that the situation as regards other forms of nutriment was by no means gratifying. He quoted "exact" figures. The Russian specialists abroad were able to establish that he had lumped the oxen together with the pigs, and also that he had reduced the head of horned cattle by transforming cows into mares—all this to the greater glory of the tsarist livestock. In Stalin's time nobody would have dared to indulge in such wangling as this. Anyone guilty of such "defeatism in the service of the counter revolution" would have been removed to the cellars of Beria and Yezhov. But now, Nikita did not mind. What he said was: "Here are the alarming facts about our agriculture. But we have taken appropriate measures, and in two or three years there will be a complete change." Sure enough, in 1955 he reported a considerable improvement, quoting figures (un-faked, this time) about the food situation in the Soviet Union.

As an expert on agriculture, Nikita also put forward his "gigantic scheme" for developing agriculture in the Soviet Union. It involved clearing a trifle of some 60,000,000 acres in Kazakhstan within a period of three years for sowing "additional cereals," besides increasing by 40,000,000 acres the area of land sown with maize—this within a period of three to five years—to feed the "additional cattle." With these objects in view, a vigorous campaign was launched. In all fairness to Nikita, it must be said that he did not take offense when another agricultural expert, who did not belong to the party but who knew a great deal about corn, reminded him that corn needs a temperate climate, and that the isotherms in the Soviet Union therefore limited the regions where it could be sown. He found the answer to this a month later. He said: we intend cultivating corn for cattle and not for human beings, so that it does not need to ripen. Cattle are just as satisfied with the green corn-stalks as with the ripe grains.

Yes, replied the expert, but these stalks ought to be stored in silos, and we have no silos. Of course, we can build them, although that may take some time. But even if we are satisfied with the green stalks, we can extend the cultivation of corn northward by only a few more degrees of latitude. That would give us about 6,000,000–10,000,000 acres together. What about your 40,000,000 acres? A week later Nikita retorted in the journal of the ministry of agriculture:

In the U.S.A. cattle are fed on freshly gathered corn-stalks. Hence we could sow corn even in the Arctic tundra, and if necessary we could warm the soil with infra-red rays.

But just fancy corn being cultivated in the tundra by hothouse methods. If the cattle were fed with this corn, the price of meat in the Soviet Union would be at least four times as much as on the world market.

Not that this worried the impulsive Nikita. Although he repudiated the dictatorial basis of Stalin's régime, his principle of personal control and his Asiatic despotism, he was still saturated to the marrow with the same régime's principle of propaganda:

Capture the imagination of the masses by whatever means you can. Make them believe that nothing is impossible in the Soviet Union, that the technique of a socialist state is capable of rising above anything, even the laws of nature.

XIV

THE STRUGGLE FOR STALIN'S SUCCESSION—II

Nikita did not merely boost the clearing of Kazakhstan and the sowing of corn in the arctic tundra. He exploited to the utmost the political situation brought about by the arrest of Beria, for the purpose of emerging from his anonymity in the secretariat of the central committee and becoming its first secretary. This occurred in August 1953, at a plenary meeting of the party central committee.

Beria had been defeated by the Khrushchev-Bulganin coalition. This victory caused considerable concern among the Soviet bureaucrats in the departments dealing with industry, finance and transport. Of all the bureaucrats, they were the most numerous—and the most powerful, too, for they had state financial resources at their disposal. The soviet press had revealed that a number of party secretaries in the provincial areas were receiving a percentage from industrial undertakings and even from the State bank. In those areas, too, there had been a certain amount of intermingling between these bureaucrats and the "apparatchiki."

Mikoyan, the most eminent representative of these finance bureaucrats (known as the "economists"), had become the "first deputy president of the council" after the arrest of Beria, but this was not enough. Further concessions to the "economists" had to be made. Nikita, always a nimble tactician, had met them more than halfway at a plenary meeting of the central committee. At this meeting they had engineered a decision by which the committee passed a resolution to "confer upon Comrade Khrushchev the title of first secretary of the central committee of the communist party." The new secretary thereupon raised no objection to a "new structure of the budget of the Soviet Union."

What exactly did all this amount to?

When the first five-year plan was started in 1929, Stalin formulated the principle of "the preponderance of heavy industry," an idea borrowed from Yuri Pyatakov, the theoretician of the five-year plan, who was shot in 1937. What differentiates the Soviet Union and soviet society from every other country is its interest, not to increase the material advantages accruing directly from production, but to bring about an increase which causes socialist patterns to become prominent, and which provides a guarantee against any imminent capitalistic aggression. This is secured by means of heavy industry.

Stalin's directives were followed with the utmost stringency. Between 1929 and 1953 the government of the Soviet Union sank the following amounts:

in heavy industry..................730.5 billion roubles
in light industry.....................77.5 billion roubles

From these figures it will be seen that the amount sunk in

heavy industry was 9.5 times greater than that sunk in light industry.

Now the plenary meeting of the central committee which conferred upon Nikita the title of first secretary decided upon a new relationship between the finances of heavy and light industry in 1954. The amounts sunk for that year were:

in heavy industry.....................90.5 billion roubles
in light industry ....14.0 billion roubles

Here the preponderance of heavy industry over light industry is represented by a ratio of 6.5 to 1.

Everybody on the committee, Nikita included, voted for this new arrangement, which was suggested by Saburov, president of the State planning department. Saburov, a friend of Mikoyan, enjoyed the favor of Malenkov as well. He had been trained at the Moscow Technological College, and he owed his career to Malenkov, his former fellow-student there.

The "new structure" aroused enormous enthusiasm among the "economists" because it meant reducing the manufacture of machine tools, armored cars, aircraft, etc., and making refrigerators, touring cars and wireless sets available in the shops. The point to note here is, that the "economists," though earning large incomes in the State service, derived little benefit from them. For all practical purposes one-half of these amounts remained frozen, since there was nothing they could buy in the shops. But henceforward they would be able to buy cars, refrigerators and so on, without having to wait for months or even years.

At the same plenary meeting Malenkov had made another proposal, by which there was to be an increase in the supply of ordinary consumer goods, such as textiles—the main item —and footwear, clothing, hosiery, etc., and also the import into the Soviet Union of certain foodstuffs previously not obtainable in the shops there.

For this purpose a sum amounting to about 50,000,000 roubles was made available, in gold and hard currencies, from the special reserve in the State bank of the Soviet Union. In this way, not only the privileged men in high places, but the underprivileged, too, could obtain a share of textiles, footwear and foodstuffs. The new first secretary of the central committee raised no objection to this. He had quickly realized that the "economists" were not going to be satisfied merely with the concession which had been made to them. While Mikoyan, their representative, was making fiery speeches, in which he promised every citizen of the Soviet Union that he would be able to buy "two pairs of boots, a suit of clothes, an extra pair of trousers and fifty yards of textiles a year," it was being whispered in the provincial regions that Malenkov was the real champion of the underprivileged, and that he ought to replace Khrushchev, the "khokhol" ("forelock," a nickname for a Ukrainian), as first party secretary.

The secretariat and the presidium of the central committee began to show signs of flurry. Ponomarenko, the former secretary in White Russia, who was younger and even more go-ahead than Nikita, was hatching a plot against his boss, and certain members of the presidium—Saburov, Shvernik, Mikoyan and even Voroshilov—were inclined to support him. The 1954 plenary meeting of the central party committee went against Nikita. Reference was made there to his "preposterous plan" for corn, and to the "scatter-brained clearing of the soil" in Kazakhstan. On the other hand, the new structure of the budget and the soft-peddling of the priority for heavy industry met with approval.

Obviously there was danger ahead, and Nikita was well aware of it. He saw, too, that the next meeting of the central committee, in January 1955, might well bring matters to a head by a maneuver to oust him in favor of Malenkov. He also knew that Ponomarenko was busily corresponding with the local provincial secretaries and several of his friends. There was, too, some veiled talk about "strengthening the secretariat of the central committee."

Counter-measures would have to be taken. Nikita took them.

He consolidated his alliance with Bulganin, which had come about during the struggle against Beria. He extended his contacts with the military authorities, who were alarmed by the great reductions in the expenditure for heavy industry and war industry, and by the "squandering" of the special reserve in the State bank, which was earmarked mainly for purposes of war.

Nikita also decided to have recourse to the press. This was an innovation in the very home of the dictatorship of the communist party. The first secretary of the central committee was actually appealing to the press for help in his attack on his central committee colleagues. Shepilov, the editor of *Pravda*, who was one of Nikita's supporters, published an article couched in menacing terms. It was a kind of warning. He reminded his readers that "the traitors Bukharin, Rykov, Tomsky and Co. had opposed the priority for heavy industry." The implication of the warning was clear. A word to the wise.

Nikita knew quite well that Malenkov would never dare to risk an open conflict. The president of the council, "bourgeoisized" after his second marriage with an actress named Helena Khrushchev (no relation to Nikita), and also in a bad state of health, was not the kind of man to rush into a free fight. The object of Shepilov's warning was to let him know that his "persistence in heresy" might cost him dear.

But Nikita was not satisfied with a mere campaign in *Pravda*, *The Communist* and other papers published under the auspices of the press and propaganda section of the central committee. He transmitted through Susslov, the head of this section, one of Bulganin's men and a former political commissar at Tukov's headquarters in 1941, a circular to the local committees. It was there insisted that "the campaign against the anti-Marxist error of reinforcing light industry must be conducted in an energetic manner." The local secretaries understood what Nikita was driving at. They were only too familiar with the technique of purges, and they were scared by the speed with which Beria, a close associate of Stalin, had been liquidated. Under these circumstances they could no longer afford to support a "heretical thesis." They would have to recant, and also attack those who had inspired the "heretical theses." Such were the standards of behavior which the Stalin régime had bequeathed to the functionaries of the party mechanism.

At the beginning of the autumn of 1954 the presidium of the central committee had to deal with the question of renewing the treaty with Mao-Tse-Tung, which had been signed by Stalin and Molotov in 1950 and would lapse in March 1955. Nikita and Bulganin exploited the resulting debate to suggest that an extraordinary delegation of the central committee should be sent to China for the purpose of drafting there the general outlines of a new treaty. Stalin had always refrained from returning the visit which Mao-Tse-Tung, president of the Chinese popular republic, had paid to the Soviet Union, and this had offended Mao. After Stalin's death, the Soviet Union could no longer afford to treat China as an underling. Hence the proposal to send a delegation there, with authority to conduct the negotiations and make decisions on the spot. This was Nikita's idea, and the delegation was to comprise four members of the presidium: Nikita himself, Bulganin, minister of war, Mikoyan, the representative of the soviet economy, and Susslov, head of the propaganda and press department.

Nikita's suggestion was accepted by the central committee. Nobody was surprised that Molotov, minister of foreign affairs, was not a member of the delegation. Mao had made no secret of his dislike for Molotov, who had conducted the negotiations with the Chinese in 1949–50 in the condescending manner of an overlord towards a retainer.

In October 1954, then, Nikita, Bulganin, Mikoyan and Susslov started for China. They were to be away for one month, but it was three months before they returned. They did not waste their time, however. After having agreed that Russia should evacuate Port Arthur, Dairen and the Manchurian railway, they quickly arranged the winding-up of the mixed Russo-Chinese companies by transferring their assets to China. They had already approached the question of a new loan to China, when Chu-Teh and Chou-En-Lai brought up a matter which was very embarrassing for Moscow. It concerned the machines and machine tools removed by the Russians from China to the Soviet Union in 1945, as well as railway material which had been treated in the same manner. This might involve a Chinese claim of as much as one billion gold roubles.

A settlement proved difficult. The Chinese discussed their claim in a friendly spirit, but their attitude was unmistakably firm. They insisted on a clear-cut reply. The Russians must either restore the machinery which had been transferred to the Soviet Union, or else make a cash payment representing its full value. After a long and somewhat trying discussion, a compromise was reached. The Chinese submitted what they described as a reasonable assessment of their losses. The Russians agreed to supply China with "the most modern equipment" at a rate which was also described as reasonable, up to a value representing one-third of the amount of the Chinese claim. In order to discharge the remainder of their debt, the Russians were to provide technical aid in the building of Chinese plants and factories, besides setting up a series of industrial plants, and constructing two railways, one on the Ulan-Batteor-Peking route, and the other linking the province of Hsing-Kiang in Chinese Turkestan with the Soviet Union and Central and Southern China.

Nikita and Bulganin left Peking for the Soviet Union in December 1954, but they did not return to Moscow direct. They travelled through the Russian seaboard province and Eastern Siberia. They visited also North Eastern Siberia, the mouths of the rivers Yana, Indiguirka, Kolyma and Lena, the gold-mines and the Arctic islands, where installations were in progress for atomic experiments and the launching of long-distance teleguided weapons. Wherever they went, it was Nikita who did the talking. Bulganin, who was tired and also unwell as a result of the banquets at Peking, spoke but seldom. As was his custom, Nikita delivered high-flown speeches, full of promises which led his hearers to believe that a good time was coming very shortly and that the end of the "five-year fast" was at hand. In the province of Magadan, which not long before had still been a huge concentration camp, but where thousands of ex-convicts were now working at the extraction of gold, Nikita took part in a grand ball in the chief town. After having drunk deep he made a speech which he concluded by saying:

Citizens, let us forget the past. I suggest that you should confer upon me the title of honorary convict.

XV

THE RESIGNATION OF MALENKOV

On reaching Moscow, Nikita proceeded to readjust the secretariat of the central committee. He first of all eliminated Ponomarenko, a dangerous rival who went so far as to refer to "all that humbug about clearing the soil in Kazakhstan." With an irony which was typically Ukrainian, Nikita arranged for Ponomarenko, "our young and energetic comrade," to be sent to Kazakhstan, of all places, as first secretary of the regional party committee.

The number of communists in Kazakhstan had increased enormously ever since the presidium of the central committee had decided to send 100,000 party members there, "to intensify the local activities." Ponomarenko thus found himself at the head of one of the most extensive communist organizations. His friends in the presidium, of whom Malenkov was the chief, could do nothing to stop this transfer. Nikita knew full well that, after a few months, it would be possible to charge Ponomarenko with failing to get the soil cleared, and that would settle his hash. That was Stalin's method of procedure, but whereas Stalin's object was the execution of his victims, Nikita's aim was merely to dash their careers in the party. As regards Ponomarenko, a few months after his arrival in Kazakhstan he was relieved of his functions, on the ground that he was "inefficient," whereupon he was sent to Warsaw and appointed ambassador of the Soviet Union in Poland.

Shatalin, another central committee secretary, was sent to Vladivostok, and was then transferred to the island of Sakhalin, which under Nicholas II had been a penal settlement, "the Russian Cayenne." The remaining secretaries simply disappeared from Moscow without leaving any clue to their whereabouts. Nikita then appointed secretaries—Aristov, Breynev and Byelayev—who were unswerving devotees of his.

The ground was now ready for the launching of an offensive against Malenkov. The removal of Malenkov had been decided upon for purely personal considerations arising from the struggle for power. These considerations were not in the least connected with the home or foreign policy of the Soviet Union. The deviation resulting from light industry was merely a pretext, as the budget for 1954 had been passed by the presidium of the central committee in a body.

Nikita quite realized that the resignation of Malenkov, if and when it became an accomplished fact, would create quite a stir inside and outside the Soviet Union. Malenkov had already embarked on his policy of friendliness towards foreign countries. He indicated that Soviet Russia would be prepared to agree to the reunification of Germany, on condition that the future fourth Reich remained neutralized.

Malenkov's policy favoring light industry had made him extremely popular in the Soviet Union. If the marshals and generals could be won over to Nikita's cause, the higher officers and some of those of lower rank, who sympathized with

Malenkov's light industry policy, would follow the example of their chiefs.

However, Nikita cautiously tried out a preparatory campaign. He declared that "the masses had the prior claim to benefit by the resources of the State." He suggested a far-reaching wage increase. This increase was effected, but within very restricted limits. Nikita then promptly turned his attention to something else. He announced that the homes of rest and the sanatoria in Southern Russia, the Crimea, the Caucasus and the Ukraine were henceforward "to be reserved on a priority basis, for the lower categories of wage earners."

Another decision on similar lines was that the Kremlin should be open to visitors. All the high functionaries of party and State who had their living quarters there were to be accommodated elsewhere. This decision really originated with Malenkov, who had suggested it to the presidium in April 1953. As the masses knew nothing about this, however, it was easy for Nikita to claim credit for it. A reduction of prices was also introduced by decree, and this gained much popularity for Nikita.

As regards foreign countries, Nikita had made a special point of granting numerous talks and interviews to foreign journalists in Moscow. Unlike Stalin, who was an adept at play-acting (he was a keen admirer of Talleyrand and Macchiavelli), Nikita is a plain, blunt man with little capacity for pretense when talking politics to foreigners. This, together with his loquacity, tended to create a wrong impression in the minds of even those foreign journalists with a close knowledge of the Soviet Union. For example, Harrison Salisbury, who certainly does not lack insight, described Nikita as an "arrant chatterbox." He also expressed the view that he would never be capable of playing the leading part, and that he would soon be out of the running. At this very moment Nikita was making ready for the ousting of Malenkov.

He was doing so with a skill from which the greatest experts at overthrowing governments in the parliamentary countries could learn a trick or two.

Beria had been got rid of by a kind of pronunciamento, but to achieve the same result with Malenkov it would be necessary to secure a regular vote at a plenary meeting of the central committee of the party which was to take place at the end of January 1955. Nikita was so pleased that he could not afford to risk failure at this meeting. If he failed, he might lose his position as first secretary, besides being accused of attempting to impair the principle of co-operation between colleagues. He therefore had to ascertain how the voting would go on this occasion, and to cope with the problem of floating votes, which was a very real one.

Now the regional committees of Sverdlovsk, Gorky, Saratov, Vologda, Stalingrad, Kalinin, Voronezh and the republic of Karelia, had expressed their "deep gratitude to Comrade Malenkov for having brought about a real co-operation between colleagues in the party leadership." This was in December 1954.

It should further be explained that the officers of the high naval command, beginning with Admiral Kuznetzev, bore a grudge against the "brass hats" of the land army, who, since the fall of Beria, were being treated with the utmost favor. The state security authorities had discovered pamphlets in the fortress of Kronstadt containing references to Stalin's "testament," and asking what had become of Basil Stalin. This was the son of Stalin, who had acted very suspiciously when Stalin's "testament," which afterwards proved to be a forgery, turned up in Moscow. As a result of this, Basil was exiled to Central Asia, where he became seriously ill and, it was rumored, did not recover.

The attitude on the part of the navy made it imperative for Nikita to take suitable measures. He appointed a new

political controller of the navy, and for this post he selected
Major-General Kornyenko, a young Ukrainian who was a
distant relation of his. Kornyenko, who took his duties very
seriously, soon began to hold frequent conferences. He also
drew up reports and issued "statements" about the new trend
of the communist party. In addition, he started a campaign
of "self-criticism," a favorite method in the Soviet Union
for bringing down opponents in high places. This caused the
rank and file to simmer with indignation. They cast asper-
sions on their commanding officers, and this provided
Bulganin, the minister of war, with a pretext for transferring
the admirals and the top naval officers to other stations. They
thus had problems enough of their own, without concerning
themselves with the question of a possible change in Malenkov's status.

In the meantime Nikita, for the benefit of foreign countries, had begun to boost his future second-in-command, Bulganin. He is one of the best administrators in the Soviet Union
and a first-rate expert on financial and monetary questions.
Unlike Nikita, he is imperturbable, and the kind of man who
acts on the principle that language has been given to us to
conceal our thoughts.

Before Malenkov actually "resigned," Bulganin was already granting interviews to foreign journalists, who were
charmed by his personality. He has the attractive appearance
of an intellectual, of a member of one of the liberal profes-
sions. His manner is jovial and he is a good conversationalist,
fond of talking about peace and a wide measure of under-
standing among nations. Such knowledge as he possesses of
English, French and German he owes to the tuition of his
wife, who is a teacher in a Moscow girls' school. He prefers
the company of actresses, film-stars, dancers and authors.

The nature of his career can be judged by the fact that he
has been lord mayor of Moscow, president of the State bank,

and president of the federative republic of Russia. During
the war he was political commissar of the politbureau, and
subsequently commander-in-chief of occupied Austria.
Strangely enough, Stalin conferred upon him the title of
marshal, and he became minister of war, without ever having
been a soldier. Foreigners found him very impressive, far
more so than Malenkov, an ungainly provincial bureaucrat
with an irregular mongoloid face.

Having reassured foreign opinion by exploiting Bulganin's
social assets, Nikita proceeded with his preparations for removing Malenkov from his position as president of the council and for inflicting a decisive blow upon his prestige in
Soviet Russia. He conferred more and more with General
Moskalenko, head of the Moscow garrison and commandant
of the Kremlin. The MVD troops, although now placed under
Moskalenko's jurisdiction, were not absolutely trustworthy.
There were quite a number of officers who compared present conditions unfavorably with those when Beria was alive,
and many of them were his fellow-countrymen or his friends
to whom he had given a helping hand.

Kruglov, the new minister of the interior, was on permanent bad terms with Lunyev, his deputy, who had been one
of the judges at Beria's trial. Although the ill-feeling between
them was of a personal character, Kruglov resented the fact
that Lunyev had helped to condemn Beria.

On January 20, 1955, Bulganin, who was minister of war,
issued instructions that the MVD troops were to go on ma-
neuvers, and they left for Kaluga. The Kremlin was occupied
by the guards regiment of the 3rd division, which had taken
part in the Battle of Moscow in 1941.

At the end of January 1955 the plenary meeting of the central committee of the communist party took place. The chief
item on the agenda was the budget for 1955. The president
of the council submitted his report. Malenkov felt that

trouble was brewing, and cautiously proposed that the ratio between the sums invested in heavy and light industry should be 6.5 to 1, the same as in the previous year.

This was the signal for launching the attack. Malenkov's "deviation" was plain for all to see. Speakers inveighed against "the incompetence of the head of the government" and his "political weakness." Allusions were made to "a blow leveled at the five-year plan." Mikoyan, who had changed sides and was now acting with Nikita, clinched matters thus:

"With Comrade Malenkov's budget we shall not be able to fulfil the commitments which we signed at Peking. Do you want to see a repetition of the Belgrade business at Peking? Do not forget that sixty per cent of our heavy industry is in Siberia, near the Chinese frontier."

By a motion, the wording of which Mikoyan had drawn up, the plenary meeting rejected the Malenkov budget. The sums invested in heavy industry were increased "so as to make it possible to deliver machines and machine tools to China and to maintain the socialist character of the five-year plan." Zveryev, the minister of finance, was instructed to present the new budget at the meeting of the supreme soviet which would be held at the beginning of February 1955. This indirect vote of censure upon the president of the council concluded the plenary meeting.

Nikita was too skilful a tactician to raise openly the question of Malenkov's resignation. The vote of the supreme soviet would be secret, and the result of it might be unexpected. Nor would it be easy to fake the voting, as only full members of the committee, numbering one hundred and twenty-five, are entitled to vote. (The deputy members, of whom there are one hundred and eleven, have only consultative rights.) Nikita and Bulganin, now in close partnership, therefore decided to "negotiate" the resignation, and Mikoyan was called in to negotiate with Malenkov. He succeeded in his mission by adopting a method hitherto unknown to the Soviet Union. He approached Malenkov's wife, using as an intermediary Madam Bulganin, who was an old friend of Madam Malenkov. Thus, the methods of the Directoire were revived in the Soviet Union.

Malenkov agreed to resign. He was given a definite promise that he would continue to be a member of the presidium of the central committee. On his part, he was to make a statement involving "self-criticism" and admitting that he was "incompetent." In his letter of resignation to the supreme soviet Malenkov duly explained the reasons for the step he was taking. He not only admitted that he was "incompetent," but added that he was "responsible for the failure of soviet agriculture, the shortage of cereals, meat, etc."

Nikita could now sleep peacefully. If at any time in the future Malenkov were to make trouble, there would be his "confession," all cut and dried, for a "crime" punishable by execution. Malenkov could also sleep peacefully. He had given a pledge that he had surrendered, and this constituted a guarantee for him, in accordance with the principles of the Stalin school of human relationships.

XVI

THE KHRUSHCHEV-BULGANIN PARTNERSHIP

Bulganin was appointed president of the council in place of Malenkov. The Khrushchev-Bulganin partnership was now in full swing. The successful pair behaved in a very restrained manner. They paraded their complete lack of any personal animosity towards their victim, and on the very next day after his resignation they were seen arm-in-arm with Malenkov at the Bolshoy Theatre. Russians and foreigners alike were amazed by this display, unique in the annals of Soviet Russia. The top dog, after having ousted his rival, took his arm to accompany him to the theatre, instead of escorting him to the cellars of the MVD.

But behind this piece of comradely make-believe, a backstairs scrimmage had been drawing to an end. The resignation of Malenkov and the rise of Nikita had been followed by the promotion of a number of admirals and marshals of armored vehicles, aircraft and artillery (a higher percentage than in July 1953), so as not to intensify the ill-feeling between the land army and the navy.

The members of the communist party also came in for quite a substantial bonus. Henceforward, party members could no longer be arrested, even if charged with a non-political offense, without the previous consent of their respective party committee. This arrangement had been in force at the time of Lenin, but Stalin had done away with it on the eve of the Big Purge, or, to be more exact, in 1934, the year in which Kirov was assassinated. Since then the GPU had full authority to arrest communists without any formal procedure. Nikita was anxious to show that he was reverting to the epoch of Lenin and that the "days of the Great Fear and the Big Purges" under Stalin were over.

For the ordinary citizen it was announced that a penal code would be published at an early date (as a matter of fact it was issued only quite recently). This code would furnish "guarantees of procedure": the presence of defending counsel at the examination of the defendant and a marked reduction in the penalties for "counter-revolutionary" activities, a charge which accounted for seventy-five per cent of the inmates of the concentration camps. It was further announced that there would be a reduction in the penalties for other crimes, and a *nolle prosequi* in the case of certain offenses which, under Stalin, had meant three to five years in a concentration camp. A supervision of judicial procedure and the review of thousands of cases of counter-revolutionary activities were also foreshadowed.

A new trend now made itself felt in the provincial and rural areas. A change of tone could be discerned in books and literary periodicals. Literature, it should be emphasized, plays a unique part in the Soviet Union. As there is no press free of control, it is mainly in literature that the effects of a new direction in politics must be looked for. Thus, in the

Literary Gazette, a very influential paper which enjoys the patronage of Nikita and Susslov, there was a short story by an author named Zyemlyak, the chief character in which was the chairman of a "kolkhoz." Here is an example of the logical manner in which he is allowed to argue:

Our "kolkhoz" has a reserve fund of more than a million roubles. But we have no tractors of our own. We have to borrow tractors from the MTS.[1] Why are the "kolkhozy" not allowed to buy their own tractors? Cars are sold to private persons in towns and cities. Why not sell tractors to the "kolkhozy"? We are tired of being exploited by the MTS.

Now the publication of a short story expressing such ideas as this in the Soviet Union has a political significance which deserves the closest attention. For what it means is that Nikita the only true begetter of the "garden city" scheme, and the man who, while Stalin was alive, was all for the transformation of the "kolkhoz" dweller into a "rural proletarian," was now favoring the whimsical notion that the "kolkhozy" should be emancipated.

After having seen to it that a turning-point was reached in the Soviet Union, Nikita launched an offensive for the purpose of relaxing international tension. This offensive was of prime importance to the dual partnership. Stalin's personal dictatorship had been psychologically favored by the fear of "capitalist aggression" against the Soviet Union. This fear had its roots in Lenin's dogma of "the capitalist encirclement of the first socialist state," and also in a constant factor in the history of Russia, the country of the steppes, without strategic obstructions, where every trace of smoke on the vast horizon might be the first sign of an enemy invasion.

[1] MTS = "Machinery and Tractor Station." These stations, which are, of course, State concerns, loan tractors to the "kolkhozy" at exorbitant rates. They are monopoly undertakings, and are actually able to pay off the cost of their equipment in three years.

Having defeated Trotsky, Stalin exploited this fear-complex to consolidate his personal dictatorship as a challenge to the capitalistic and fascist world, whose sole aim was "the destruction of the first socialist state." In Soviet Russia, which, as the result of Stalin's dogma concerning "socialism in a single country" had once more become practically a nationalist state, the needs of external security overrode all other considerations. In an absolutist state personal dictatorship is the only means of establishing power on the firmest possible basis. In this way Stalin became the living symbol of the Soviet Union. All those who were his personal enemies became *ipso facto* the enemies of the state, traitors.

This Cæsarean principle, which may be regarded as a fairly normal item in a dictator's armory, was supplemented in the case of Stalin by certain features peculiar to him. It was not for nothing that he had once studied at a seminary, where he had imbibed the idea that the head of the church was infallible and had a perfect right to interfere in every domain, scientific, literary, moral and so forth. To make matters worse, Stalin was a shadowy, cruel, treacherous person, whose heredity was tainted by his father's alcoholism.[1] He suffered, too, from an inferiority complex, due to his contact with the personality of a man like Trotsky. He was a native of Gori, an Asiatic village, where the law of the Georgian vendetta was handed down from father to son for dozens of generations. Before sending his enemies to their death (and it should be remembered that they were Lenin's most distinguished followers) he forced them to abase themselves publicly, while he, hidden in a recess behind a drawn curtain, gloated over what he saw. In order to indemnify himself for his inferiority complex, he did not limit his dictatorship to the Cæsarean principle. He also set himself up as the successor of Marx, the foremost architect, the foremost mathe-

[1] This was first revealed by B. Suvarin in his book *Stalin*.

matician, the foremost literary critic, the foremost philologist, the foremost biological expert. In a word, he made himself infallible.

Nikita made no attempt to emulate these attainments after his victory over Malenkov. He did not feel any need to do so. He was sprung from those unruly vagrants who elected their "atamans" only for a time and for some specified task. Their ataman was merely "primus inter pares." If he showed the slightest inclination to become a personal dictator, any Cossack whatever had the right to give the alarm, summon the "rada" or Ukrainian assembly to the market-place, and accuse the ataman publicly of trying to seize dictatorial power. If this accusation was considered to be well-founded, the ataman was driven out of Cossack territory, and sometimes he was beaten to death with cudgels.

Nikita was well aware that any attempt to restore personal power would rouse fierce opposition, and that any such opposition would prove to be far more effective than at the time when Stalin was struggling against his enemies. The members of the presidium of the central committee remembered the fate of their colleagues in the politbureau on the eve of the establishment of Stalin's personal dictatorship. But the essential point was that Nikita had no intention of aspiring to anything of that kind. He was a hard task master when there was work to be done, but after work he quickly unbent. He would make jokes, and gossip for hours at a time with his subordinates. Anyone could even venture to tell an anecdote about him. Such an act of *lèse-majesté* would have been quite unthinkable under Stalin.

Nikita, the wily Ukrainian, however, was alive to the fact that it was not enough to scout the idea of aiming at personal dictatorship. As long as the psychological conditions which had favored the Cæsarism of Stalin persisted, a reversion to the past was always a possibility to beware of. This was the real reason which urged Nikita and his presidium to embark on an offensive for the purpose of relaxing international tension. But he did not propose to make any expensive concessions to end the cold war which had been provoked by Stalin, and which had brought about a psychosis in the United States, as well as the fear of war among the people in the Soviet Union. Such concessions as he could offer the opposite side had only a restricted scope. The monopoly of power held by the communist party in the Soviet Union would have to stay. The "apparatchiki," the most influential among the soviet bureaucrats, would not tolerate any curtailment of their privileges. The complete State control of the national economy in the national economy in the Soviet Union would also have to be retained, together with its resulting monopoly of foreign trade and the drift towards autarchy. The break with the "capitalist sector" of the world market would have to continue. Nor could Nikita liberate the "glacis of security" in Central Europe—the satellite countries. The military authorities sternly set their face against anything of that kind.

The cold war could end only in an armistice—in the establishment of a demilitarized zone where the opposing sides were in contact with each other; that is to say, in Austria and Germany.

In March 1955 Nikita called a small conference to prepare for the relaxation of international tension. The report on this subject was not presented by Molotov. He had asked to be excused, and tendered his resignation, which was accepted in June 1955. The report was handled by Dimitri Shepilov, secretary of the central committee and future minister of foreign affairs. The new foreign policy was to take shape under Nikita's auspices.

XVII

FROM THE JOURNEY TO BELGRADE
TO THE ASIATIC JOURNEY

Shepilov was born in 1907. He is an agricultural expert, a former student at the party high school, professor at the Karl Marx-Friedrich Engels-Lenin-Stalin college, author of several dissertations on sociology, philosophy and history, and is regarded in the Soviet Union as an outstanding authority on foreign affairs. Secretary of the central committee, he was also president of the foreign affairs commission of the supreme soviet. He was on close terms with Nikita who thought highly of him. We have seen that as editor of *Pravda*, Shepilov was involved in the campaign to overthrow Malenkov. He is the archtype of the soviet intellectual. He greatly relishes his position as *éminence grise* of the first secretary of the party, who had chosen him to report on the relaxation of international tension.

As a matter of fact, the choice was not exactly a happy one.

It has already been mentioned that Shepilov studied at the party high school, which has turned out several generations of left-wing oppositionists with leanings towards syndicalism. Most of them, notably Perepetchko, Yan, Maretzky and Ryutin, disappeared during the Big Purge. On account of his youth, Shepilov was lucky enough not to be mixed up directly in these activities. He was under the personal protection of Voroshilov, and withdrew to a provincial area to prepare a dissertation on the colonial question, which was subsequently published in the *Bulletin of the Karl Marx-Friedrich Engels College*. It dealt mainly with the 1916 controversy between Lenin and Kievsky, the pseudonym of Platonov. At that time Lenin was in Switzerland, editing *The Social Democrat*. Kievsky, following the lead of Rosa Luxemburg, maintained that "once the socialist revolution had achieved success in one of the belligerent countries, the problem of the national liberation of the Asiatic countries, and in general, the colonial countries, would be solved automatically. There would be no need to carry on propaganda in those countries, nor to support them in their struggle."

Lenin took the view that "revolutionary propaganda ought to be launched immediately, in the form of national liberation in the colonial countries, as a means for depriving the imperialist powers of the bases from which they obtained their raw materials."

Shepilov was wholeheartedly in favor of these ideas, and "colonial Leninism" was a fundamental feature of his program. Another of Shepilov's bright ideas was to trot out a forgotten passage from volume 25, page 58 of Lenin's complete works. The passage ran as follows:

All nations will ultimately adopt socialism. This is the inevitable trend of History. But they will not reach this stage by the same route. Each one will pursue a form of democracy suited to itself, or a particular form of the dictatorship of the proletariat. And then, too, there will be nations who will follow the rhythm of socialist transformations historically appropriate to their structure and way of life.

This is an extremely dark utterance. It provides no criterion by which any given nation is to choose any particular one of the routes which are mentioned. Nor does it explain why Russia should be indefinitely subjected to "the dictatorship of the proletariat," that is to say, the monopoly of power in the hands of one single party, whereas other and more fortunate countries could do without it.

At all events, Shepilov's eclectic report was a source of the utmost satisfaction to Nikita. It enabled him to justify the slackening of the soviet pressure on the satellite countries in Central and Eastern Europe, who would continue to follow their socialist course without being under the influence of Soviet Russia. It also enabled him to make it up with Tito, who, "was following the socialist course appropriate to the historical conditions in Yugoslavia." It enabled him, too, to conclude an agreement with any capitalist country which, in the words of Shepilov, "set foot on the path of socialism" by the emergence of a popular front or of a socialist or labor government. And finally, it enabled him to start an economic and political penetration in the colonial and semi-colonial countries of Asia and Africa. All this was propped up by the slogan "Back to Leninism," which was based upon a single utterance by Lenin, as expounded by Shepilov.

Nikita is no dogmatist, but he has contrived to shape for himself what may be described as a "Leninist breast-plate," as a means of defense against any of his opponents who may attack him on account of his policy of relaxing tension. Unlike Stalin, he does not hold absolutist sway, and it was quite enough for him to become the acknowledged interpreter of Lenin, the spiritual leader of Soviet Russia.

Nikita's program for relaxing tension involved certain sacrifices on the part of Soviet Russia. One of them was the evacuation of Austria. The "emancipation" of sorts which had been granted to the satellite countries met with disapproval on the part of a group of last-ditchers, of whom Molotov was the spokesman. It was no mere chance that in March 1955, when Shepilov was expounding his ideas about relaxed tension, Molotov made a speech on the satellites. In this speech he denied that the satellites were on the "road to socialism." And General Shtemenko, former chief of the general staff, stated in a lecture to the army and navy club that the evacuation of Austria would involve strategic and political dangers.

It was only the posthumous authority of Lenin which enabled Nikita to counteract the efforts of his opponents. Accompanied by Bulganin, he set out on his crusade to preach the gospel of relaxed tension. The journey to Belgrade was the first stage. It cannot be said that it was easy for Nikita to strike the right note. His speech at Belgrade, in which he dealt with "Beria, the agent provocateur," who had caused the break with Yugoslavia, was bound to arouse the mirth of the Yugoslavs. They knew perfectly well that it was Stalin who had ordered the communist parties of the Cominform to break with them, while concurrently he had ordered Beria to "draw up the dossier of Tito the traitor." But as soon as Nikita had got this embarrassing speech off his chest, he admitted quite frankly in a private conversation with the Yugoslavs that Stalin was the chief culprit in the matter of the break with them.

This reveals an interesting trait in Nikita's character. Being of Ukrainian origin, he is completely devoid of the byzantinism which is so prevalent among the Russians. Having become a statesman, he cannot tell the truth, or at any rate, the whole truth. But in his private capacity he is at once quite willing to open up. This is something of which a man like Molotov would be utterly incapable.

The stay in Belgrade revealed certain other of Nikita's foibles which we have already noted. He took a great liking to Yugoslav shlivovitza, or plum brandy, and did full justice to it. Also, in his exuberant, hail-fellow-well-met manner which nobody could take amiss, he flirted with Jovanka Broz, Marshal Tito's handsome wife. One evening, when there was a dinner-party at the Marshal's villa on the island of Brioni, Nikita, who was not altogether sober, tried to kiss Jovanka. She laughingly dodged him. And after dancing a popular Ukrainian dance with her, he sang her an old Ukrainian serenade, a love-lorn ditty in which the moon looms large. Ukrainian is fairly close to Slovene, so that Marshal Tito and his wife managed to follow the general drift of the words, and they both roared with laughter. Mikoyan, affecting to be alarmed, asked Nikita to tell him the meaning of the song in Russian.

"You never know where you are with this fellow," added Mikoyan. "When he's had a few drinks, he's quite capable of singing something anti-communist."

They laughed louder than ever. Nikita suggested a stroll in the moonlight.

"Why, it's past midnight," said Tito. "Time to go to bed."

"Nonsense," replied Nikita. "In the Ukraine our parties never break up until we've emptied all the bottles. I'm all right here, and I'm going to stay."

After having accounted for some more bottles, he said to Mikoyan:

"When you sign a new trade and barter treaty with Comrade Tito, don't forget to add a special clause."

"What clause?" asked Tito, who wondered what was coming next.

"The treaty becomes null and void if Marshal Tito fails to barter his wife for the wife of Nikita Sergyeyevitch Khrushchev, member of the presidium of the supreme soviet."[1]

1 This is Nikita's only official title.

It was nearly three o'clock in the morning when Mikoyan and Colonel Maltchikov, of the State security service, managed to get Nikita out of Marshal Tito's villa. He strongly objected. He wanted to sleep on a settee in the dining room.

But at Geneva Nikita kept studiously in the background. He went off on his own, exploring the places of interest in and around the city. In particular, he visited the spot where Lenin used to go fishing on Sundays. And it was now Bulganin's turn to conduct the negotiations. But the conference of the Big Four produced no results to speak of. There was no agreement on Germany, no agreement on disarmament, no agreement on the atomic and hydrogen bombs. Nevertheless its psychological importance was considerable. Nikita Khrushchev, "the Taras Bulba of the Soviet Union," and Bulganin, his second-in-command, made their appearance before the Western public. They had drawn aside the veil of mystery with which Stalin had shrouded his Kremlin, and revealed the "Western countenance" of the Russian Janus, instead of the Asiatic aspect which Stalin had imprinted on his empire.

The cold war "armistice" was signed. Nikita had engineered it.

On his return from Geneva, Nikita consolidated his influence in the presidium of the central committee. Kiritchenko, his special agent in the Ukraine, had become a member of the presidium. Aristov, who, in close touch with Susslov, was to have directed the secretariat of the central committee, proved unequal to his task. Susslov then became a member of the presidium together with Kiritchenko, after having given "pledges of fidelity" to Nikita during a conference at Leningrad.

Nikita now began to make preparations for his journey to Asia, the second part of his program. At Moscow it was realized that the situation was a delicate one. India was an independent republic, but was still in the sterling area and also in the strategic area of Great Britain. Burma was a neighbor of Malaya, the most important point of the area containing the raw materials—rubber and tin—which help to bolster up the somewhat shaky British balance of payments.

Nikita did not intend to stimulate communist activity in that part of the world. What he had in mind was a trade and economic penetration which, though annoying to London, differed in no way from the normal competition of capitalist countries. Nevertheless, this journey chilled British-Soviet relations, and produced by way of a reprisal British reactions in the Near-and Middle-East, resulting in the Bagdad Pact. This, in its turn, led to deliveries of soviet armaments to the Arab countries.

XVIII

FROM THE ASIATIC JOURNEY TO
THE TWENTIETH PARTY CONGRESS

On the eve of Nikita's Asiatic journey, an article by Shepilov appeared in the press. It attracted no attention, but it was of interest, in that it gave some idea of the character of the journey. Its general purport was as follows:

"We are reverting to Leninism, and hence it is our duty to help the peoples of Asia and Africa, the colonial and semi-colonial peoples. This does not mean setting up among them a communist party, with the object of establishing an immediate dictatorship. That might merely operate to the detriment of the Soviet Union by alarming the national bourgeoisie in the colonial countries and impelling them in the direction of the U.S.A. What the Soviet Union has to do is to create permanent links with the nationalist parties and wait until industrialization establishes conditions favorable to the formation of a powerful working class and a socialist revolution."

Nikita acted on the general ideas thus expounded by his

adviser. Throughout the journey he made a special point of cracking up the historical past, the culture, the literature and the civilization as a whole, of the countries he visited. He promised them the help of the Soviet Union in the building of factories, industrial plants and railways, and this help was to be granted without strings and without red tape. He purchased the surplus stocks of rice and other redundant products which were rotting in the warehouses. He tried the national dishes and, without any reluctance, drank the native alcoholic beverages. Sometimes he even donned the national costume for a pilgrimage to holy places, and he then made speeches. Speeches without end, on all occasions, and, indeed, when there was no occasion at all.

Bulganin followed him without any marked enthusiasm. The head of the government of the Soviet Union lacks the stamina of Nikita, and the exertions of a journey in tropical countries during the height of the season were very much of an ordeal for him. Frequently he was quite exhausted, and lagged far behind his zestful first secretary. This did not worry Nikita. He was relying on his own activities. The plan of his speeches was simple. Flattery of the Asiatic masses formed their keynote. He remembered how, at the time of the Russian revolution in 1917, the orators told the muzhiks that they were "the representatives of the only true civilization." Nikita now repeated these very words. His speech at the Burmese pagoda was the oddest of them all. Speaking to a huge crowd which had gathered to listen to him, Nikita said:

"This pagoda is nearly 2,000 years old. Those who built it, your Burmese ancestors, possessed the greatest civilization in the world at that time. And yet the English have said that the Burmese of the nineteenth century were only savages. Your civilization will stand any comparison with that of the English. English civilization did not begin until 1066, at the time of Edward the Conqueror, 1,000 years after this pagoda was built."

Nikita's speech showed that he had read history books and that he remembered a number of important dates. We cannot say whether he deliberately muddled up the names of Edward the Confessor and William the Conqueror. Anyhow, his interpreter reproduced the howler, which apparently passed unnoticed by the Burmese gathered in front of the pagoda—but of course their knowledge of English history was scanty. Nikita's speech was greeted with wild applause. Demagogy had done the trick.

As soon as he was back again in Moscow, in mid-winter 1955-56, Nikita began to make ready for the twentieth congress of the Russian communist party, which was to be held in February 1956. His job now was to make absolutely certain of a majority at the congress and to work out a "new look" for the party. The latter task was to be handled by a commission, presided over by himself, and consisting of Shepilov, Mikoyan, Susslov, Bulganin, Kaganovitch and Voroshilov. Before this commission met, Nikita had completed a big re-shuffle of regional party secretaries, the purpose of which was to eliminate all those on whom he could not thoroughly rely. In the Soviet Union it is these local secretaries who have some say in the choice of delegates to the congress because they submit lists of names to the local conferences. Now some of these secretaries were, from Nikita's point of view, of doubtful loyalty. He suspected them of being pro-Ponomarenko or pro-Susslov. As we have already mentioned, Ponomarenko had been eliminated by being sent to Warsaw. Susslov, who was very popular with the army, could not be eliminated, and it therefore became necessary to remove the local secretaries.

By the beginning of January 1956 the re-shuffle of secretaries had been completed. The secretaries of the regions of

Gorky (formerly Nizhny-Novgorod), Saratov, Sverdlovsk, Stalingrad, Karelia, Irkutsk, Vologda and the Caucasus were removed and replaced by men whom Nikita could fully trust. The chief secretary at Leningrad, a certain Koslov, remained in office. He was one of Nikita's old acquaintances. The same applied to Katherine Furtzeva, the Moscow secretary, who owed her position to Nikita's influence, while Kiritchenko, Nikita's handyman, was in charge in the Ukraine. As these three regions accounted for seventy-five per cent of the delegates at the conference, Nikita's majority was beyond all doubt.

Nikita wanted to supplement the re-shuffling of secretaries by an important change within the government; he was bent on getting rid of Kruglov, the minister of the interior, a member of the central committee of the communist party and formerly Stalin's bodyguard at Teheran, Yalta and Potsdam.

After the arrest of Beria, the secret police had been transferred from the jurisdiction of the ministry of the interior to that of the State security commission, presided over by General Serov, one of Nikita's men. But the ministry of the interior had retained under its control quite a number of important bodies, such as the municipal police, and it also supervised soviet elections. Moreover, Kruglov was a friend of Ponomarenko, and, although he had helped to arrest Beria, he had kept away from the court which had condemned Beria to death—Lunyev, the deputy minister of the interior, had acted as his substitute. Kruglov's removal from office confronted Nikita with yet another difficulty. The minister of the interior had been a frequent visitor to the country villa of Bulganin, whom he had known for many years.

Nikita got round all this by removing Kruglov while Bulganin was on sick leave for a month from his duties as president of the council. Dudorov, the new minister of the interior, an architect by profession and former president of the State building committee, was an old friend of Nikita. Their friendship dated back to the time when the Moscow underground railway was being built. Dudorov was also in favor with Kaganovitch and Bulganin. By his appointment, the first secretary of the party avoided any discord with the head of the government.

Having thus made sure that the rear was safe, Nikita started on the ideological preparation of a "new look" for the party. The special commission sat for nearly a month, from January 10, to February 5, 1956, before the "new look" was finally worked out. The main result of its activities was that Shepilov and Nikita between them made the following interesting discovery: "Revolutions could take place in certain countries, and under certain historically determined conditions, along peaceful lines, by the utilization of bourgeois parliaments." This discovery was based on the fact that, after the insurrection of 1917, Lenin had summoned Kerensky's constituent assembly, on the assumption that this body would ratify the "November conquests." But the meeting of the constituent assembly produced no results. Lenin was mistaken in his assumption. The constituent assembly demanded that a genuine democratic body should be set up, and was opposed to a separate peace with Germany. Lenin therefore ordered the constituent assembly to be dissolved. Nevertheless, the mere fact that Lenin had summoned a "bourgeois assembly" had shown, according to Shepilov and Nikita, that such bodies could be utilized.

The second item in the "new look" was concerned with cooperation and in due course a possible alliance with the socialists. The first soviet government in 1917 had consisted of a coalition between the bolsheviks and the left-wing social revolutionaries, a party with which Nikita had been in sympathy. Lenin had tried to rope in also Martov-Tsederbaum's menshevik internationalists, but Martov had declined to join. He had demanded a guarantee of democratic liberties.

By taking his stand upon this "precedent," Nikita thought it would be possible to include in the "new look" the principle of co-operation with the socialists in non-soviet countries. Although the experience of coalition government in Russia had produced no positive result (the left-wing social revolutionaries had rebelled against Lenin in June 1918 on account of the peace of Brest-Litovsk, which they refused to recognize), the principle of co-operation with the socialists was accepted by the special commission. It also accepted the principle of co-operation with a government which was "homogeneously socialist" or even "sincerely democratic," this decision being based on the fact that the government of Count Karoly had handed over the power in Hungary to the bolsheviks in 1919.

Shepilov's idea was that all these forms of co-operation were merely "temporary forms leading towards the dictatorship of the proletariat," which was the final aim of such co-operation. In spite of fact, the late "little father of the peoples" had likewise recognized this brand of Leninism. In 1927 he had urged the Chinese communist party to merge itself with Chiang-Kai-Shek's Kuo-Min-Tang party for the purpose of entering the Chinese government and smashing it from within. But since 1927 much water has flown under the bridges of the Yang-Tsi-Kiang and of Moscow. Still, Nikita was able to gain acceptance for his "new principle" as a reversion towards Leninism and a break with Stalinism. This break was demanded particularly by Mikoyan, the representative of the "economists" on the special commission. The "economists," the most privileged category of the soviet bureaucracy, intended to obtain some compensation for having agreed to the resignation of Malenkov. Under Stalin they could be summarily arrested by the secret police, who could

confiscate all their property at a moment's notice. We have
seen that Nikita had granted them certain privileges. The
secret police was no longer allowed to make arbitrary arrests,
and property could be confiscated only after a court ruling.
But these were concessions which they shared with all other
citizens of the Soviet Union, and they had no guarantee that
these concessions would last. Their governments, as they were
well aware, could annul today what they had granted yester-
day, as during the Stalin period. They therefore insisted on
a complete break with Stalinism, and with any of those methods of Stalinism which might prevent them, the "economists,"
from enjoying their privileges without any misgivings whatever.

Mikoyan, their spokesman, brought up this matter before
the special commission. In order to destroy Stalinism once
and for all, it became necessary to inflict a decisive, even
though posthumous, blow upon Stalin personally. It became
necessary to declare publicly that the "prodigious" Stalin had
been guilty of a vast number of the most grievous and blatant
errors; that he had brought the Soviet Union within an ace
of defeat by his policy of alliance with Hitler for the purpose
of dividing Poland between them; that he had blundered by
driving Tito into the western camp without any reason whatever; that he had been guilty of other errors, not to say crimes,
in his various purges.

Nikita had partly made amends for these errors and crimes.
But he had done so without any fuss, even by stealth, his aim
being to saddle Beria with the errors of his former boss. He
was reluctant to decide upon a sudden break. He was familiar
with the character of the Russian crowd, its traditional lack of
discipline, its craving for abstract "justice," its inclination for
anarchy. He had been among the crowds in 1917. He had witnessed their delight when Russia had got rid of all policemen
at the time of Kerensky, when no holds were barred. He had

read *The Twelve,* by Alexander Blok, the greatest Russian poet of the twentieth century, and specially part IX, which opens thus:

> The bustle of the city is hushed,
> Silence reigns above the Tower of the Neva.
> Not a single policeman left—
> Let's go on the spree, lads, even though
> There's nothing to drink.

Nikita realized that, once freedom got under way, there would be no stopping it. The "apparatchiki," the party bureaucrats, who still had a firm grip on their control of the Soviet Union, and of whom he was the fugleman, were scared of such a possibility. On the other hand, the "economists" were by no means scared of it. As in 1917, there was a clash between two groups which were to some extent related, but one of which wanted to seize power; a debate between Nikita and Mikoyan, the Trepov and the Milyukov[1] of the Soviet Union. Mikoyan demanded that there should be a complete repudiation of Stalin and Stalinism, which thwarted the crystallization of a new class, his class. Nikita would agree only to a reform of Stalinism, a half-measure. The first rift in the monolithic regime of the Soviet Union was revealed in the special commission. It was to be displayed quite openly at the twentieth congress of the communist party.

[1] Trepov was the last president of the Tsarist council in 1917. Milyukov was the head of the monarchist constitutional party, known as the cadets.

THE TWENTIETH CONGRESS

The special commission failed to reach an agreement. Mikoyan refused to budge a single inch from his demands. He had gained a measure of support from Bulganin who had now recovered from his illness. Susslov showed some reluctance to identify himself with Nikita, and Voroshilov adopted the same attitude. Shepilov and Kaganovitch gave Nikita their full support.

If Nikita had been aspiring to personal dictatorship, he could have seized the opportunity provided by the twentieth party congress to emerge from it as Stalin II. His majority at the congress had been hand-picked. But instead of involving himself in a dispute, Nikita preferred to make a compromise. He could see the danger of allowing the communist party, the people of the Soviet Union and foreign countries, to know that there was a split in the central committee and in its presidium. The lesson of 1917 had gone home. "Trepov-Khrushchev" was not going to try conclusions with "Milyukov-Mikoyan."

It was agreed that recognition should be given to the necessity of a final break with Stalinism. As regards the form which this break should assume, each group could champion its own. They had chosen the same route towards their goal, but they had not settled in advance how far they would march together. This distance was to be decided by the "historically determined situation," each faction hoping that the situation in question would operate to its particular advantage.

The compromise was reached on the assumption of a preliminary agreement about the allotment of representation in the future presidium of the central committee. Although Nikita held the majority at the congress, he was ready to leave the composition of the presidium unchanged. His only request was that there should be an increase in the number of deputy members. This was to be done by bringing in two representatives of the Asiatic republics in the Soviet Union, Kazakhstan and Uzbekistan, Shepilov, who had become the "official ideologist" to Nikita, and Katherine Furtzeva, his secretary at Moscow.

During the early part of the congress there was no indication of a serious clash between the two factions, but the rift between the rival sets of bureaucrats made itself felt in due course. In his speech, which lasted for eight hours, Nikita emphasized a few concepts held in common, such as that of cooperative leadership and the repudiation of the personality cult. He referred to the errors which this cult had occasioned, without specifying which personality he had in mind, although everyone knew it was Stalin. This was his manner of pledging himself that the Stalin dynasty would come to an end in the mausoleum on the Red Square. He made the most of the effect which this repudiation produced. The members of the congress had applauded unrestrainedly each time he entered the hall, and he finally took them up on this. He said:

"Don't applaud like that. Don't forget that you are the masters here."

Party discipline in the Soviet Union is of an extremely high standard. This remark by Nikita was enough to reduce the volume of applause very considerably. In fact, a number of delegates could be seen talking while their chiefs were delivering speeches. This would have been unthinkable when Stalin was in charge.

After having concluded the anti-Stalinism part of his speech, Nikita went on to discuss the outlook for economic development in the Soviet Union (this was to be detailed by Bulganin in his report), and the improvement of living conditions. He promised "the socialist working week" (which has since been announced as amounting to forty-six hours), and a very liberal scheme of free higher education, with study grants, allowances for students and so on. There was also to be an increase in productivity. He spoke at some length, too, about the need to improve the conditions prevailing in the "kolkhozy" (a new "kolkhoz" statue was promulgated on March 9, 1956).

With a view to winning over the "economists," Nikita promised to initiate a system of autonomy for nationalized concerns, on the lines of the Renault factories in France. This sounded very attractive. Under Tsarism an attempt had been made to pacify the progressive bourgeoisie in Russia by a policy of subsidies for industry: an economic concession had been put forward as a substitute for a proper political constitution. Nikita was now offering the same bait to the "economists." In reply Mikoyan, their representative, made a speech in which he did not mince his words. He said that the "economists" would not be satisfied with a repudiation of Stalinism, unless, first of all, steps were taken to discredit finally the man who had brought Stalinism into the world, namely, Stalin himself. They wanted the whole country to know that Stalin had made mistakes, that he had vitiated Leninism, and that he had set up a despotic Asiatic régime, thus outraging the laws of the Soviet Union, in order to settle accounts with his personal opponents. At the same time the "economists" did not intend immediately to espouse the cause of the "right-wing opposition," represented by Rykov, Bukharin and Tomsky. Here, Mikoyan was cautious. He refrained from mentioning the real opposition leaders who had been executed at Stalin's orders—Trotsky, Zinovyev, Kamenev, Radek, Piatakov, Muralov and others. He did not demand a frank and emphatic rehabilitation of these followers of Lenin. But he hinted that such a demand was by no means ruled out.

Nikita had been warned. If one day he were to set himself against the crystallization of a new privileged class in Soviet Russia, these corpses would be exhumed to discredit Stalin and to cast a slur upon the men who, in October 1952, had helped to elaborate the new party line.

Nikita saw the point. He climbed down. But he, too, had issued a warning. In the lobbies of the congress he adroitly dropped hints about the election of his friend Zhukov to the presidium of the central committee as a deputy member, which meant that the military section of soviet bureaucracy was making its appearance in the party's holy of holies, its presidium. In this way Nikita established a counterpoise to the pressure of the "economists." If this pressure became too strong, he could have recourse to an alliance with the military men by way of tackling the danger of a transfer of power from the "apparatchiki" to the "economists." The military men, the only section of soviet bureaucracy strictly national in character, could be called upon by Nikita to help him.

Mikoyan's speech aroused a tidal wave of enthusiasm at the congress. The applause was, according to the official press, "thunderous." Of course, Nikita's speeches, too, had been received in an equally "thunderous" manner. This was a survival from the Stalin tradition—official homage to the secretary of the central committee of the party, to the leading man in party and country. But in the case of Mikoyan it meant something different: homage to the man who, for the first time, had uttered officially and publicly the truth about the despotism and tyranny of Stalin. This homage had shown clearly that the sympathies of the twentieth congress, where the "apparatchiki" were represented by a majority, were moving in the direction of those who wanted to put an end, once and for all, to the legend of Stalin.

As a shrewd politician, Nikita quickly gauged the situation. Mikoyan, fugleman of the "economists," had begun his career as an "apparatchik." In 1923 he had been secretary of the party committee in the Northern Caucasus. It was quite possible that the "economists" had tried to make Mikoyan their candidate for the position of first secretary of the central committee. Nikita forestalled any such move. He decided to hold a secret session of the congress, to make known the precise and detailed reasons for the break with Stalinism. This secret session was held on the eve of the election of members of the central committee. It was to have a decisive bearing upon the history of post-Stalin Russia.

In order to link the new principle of "management by colleagues," the anti-Stalin principle in methods of organization, with the reversion to pure Leninism, Nikita first of all read the complete text of Lenin's testament, written in 1923:

Our party is an iron cohort. It should remain united and unshakable until the end of its revolutionary task.

From this point of view, the question of leadership plays a paramount part. It is not a question of having a leader who makes personal decisions and imposes his will. That would run counter to our whole philosophy and our moral principles, and could lead only towards a Napoleonic degeneration.

No, our leadership involves the need for a directive body of colleagues, set up by the central committee elected at the pan-Russian congress of the bolshevik party. This body would reach decisions by the democratic principle of a majority vote. The minority would have the right to record its opinion in a special expression of views, and in such a case, if the divergence were to be very considerable, to convene an extraordinary party congress to smooth matters out.

In order to prevent divergences from breaking up the central committee and leading to a fratricidal struggle between the bolsheviks, I have recommended the establishment of a central control commission which would serve as a buttress of unity.

This, however, would not be adequate, if the party congress did not take into consideration the qualities of the men in charge and remove those who might foment a fratricidal struggle.

At the moment there are two comrades who are the outstanding personalities among the men in charge: Stalin and Trotsky.

The secretary general of our party[1] is too uncouth in his demeanor. This, in itself, would not necessarily disqualify the rank and file of the communist party, but in a secretary-general it is quite inadmissible.

Stalin is also unprincipled in his relations with party members. He is petty-minded and jealous. He is capable of taking advantage of his position and power to settle personal accounts with other comrades. If Stalin were allowed to continue as secretary-general, the danger of a rift in the party would become imminent. For personal motives Stalin would favor such a rift, which would enable him to start a struggle against Trotsky.

I therefore recommend that Stalin should be removed from his post and replaced by another comrade who is likely to be more honest, more courteous, more considerate and more impartial in his personal relations.

As regards Trotsky, it must not be forgotten that he is not a bolshevik, although he has played an enormous part in our revolution and in the establishment of our state. He will never be a genuine bolshevik. Nevertheless, he must not be decried because of his lack of bolshevism.

Kamenev and Zinovyev are useful and influential members of the leadership. But it must not be forgotten that their errors in

[1] i.e. Stalin.

1917[1] were not due to mere chance. Nevertheless, they must not be admonished for these errors, just as Trotsky must not be admonished for his lack of bolshevism.

Bukharin and Piatakov are young members of the leadership who are very able and may prove useful.

Bukharin is a pedant and a dogmatist. Sometimes he is rather futile and inclined to make historical comparisons which are inaccurate and dangerous.[2] Piatakov is too much impressed with the importance of his position as administrator, and he imagines that all difficulties can be settled by orders from above.

This is not meant as the last word on the subject, for these two comrades are still young and they may be able to adapt themselves better to the requirements of leadership between colleagues.

After having read Lenin's testament, Nikita spoke for another three hours about the errors of Stalin. He first of all pointed out that Stalin had fallen a prey to his own anti-Marxist theory of personal power, that this theory had profoundly changed him in a psychological respect, that he had ended by believing in his own infallibility, and that he had lumped together all those who were not in agreement with him, even over quite secondary matters, as enemies of party and people, and foreign agents.

According to Nikita, Beria and the other heads of the secret police were merely the "exploiters and henchmen of Stalin's obsession with unlimited personal power." Prompted by their own interests, and desiring to gain a hold on party and

[1] In November 1917 Kamenev and Zinovyev were opposed to the revolution, and an article by them against Lenin was published in Gorky's paper *The New Life*. Later on, they apologized, and Lenin bore them no ill-will whatever.

[2] This refers to a speech by Bukharin, in which he compared the bolshevik party to the Order of the Jesuits, of all things. He said:

"Our party resembles the Order of the Jesuits, founded by a saint who was a soldier, a politician, an organizer and, above all, a man of intelligence.

"The Jesuits succeeded in serving the church in a manner completely devoid of vanity and divorced from personal interests.

"I do not hesitate to make this comparison. We are the red Jesuits, in the best sense of the word."

state, the political police, who were not, and could not be, controlled, trumped up charges of conspiracy, and shot thousands of functionaries of party and state, officers and engineers. It had taken Stalin nearly two years to discover that Yezhov was a sadist and a maniac, after he had already wiped out the pick of the army command in 1938, on the eve of the war, thus putting the Soviet Union in mortal peril in 1941.

The same political police had led Stalin astray in 1940, on the eve of the German invasion. Dekanozov, the assistant of Beria, had been appointed ambassador at Berlin, and, with all the resources of the intelligence service at his disposal, had asserted that Hitler would never attack the Soviet Union, and that the concentration of German troops on the frontier was nothing but bluff. Stalin unreservedly took his word for this, in spite of the information collected by the secret service, which was more trustworthy, and was confirmed by the military attaché of the Soviet Union at Berlin, as well as by a report made to Stalin in May 1941 by the British Ambassador in Moscow.

Stalin was so cock-sure of his own analysis of the international situation, according to which Hitler would never dare to attack the Soviet Union and start a full-scale war on two fronts, that he pooh-poohed the evidence of a German refugee, a soldier named Wilhelm Korpik, who deserted from the German army on the night of June 21, 1941. This soldier had warned the officers of the Red Army that a general attack had been decided upon, and that it was to be launched on June 22 at four o'clock. He mentioned that this order had just been read out to the regiments.

Stalin refused to take this warning seriously. He had received the statement by private telephone from the commanding officer of that particular sector, and had then given orders that the "deserter who supplied misleading information" was to be shot, although he belonged to the working classes and had been a member of the German communist party in the Schlesischer Bahnhof quarter of Berlin.

The outbreak of war found Stalin in a state of utter demoralization. It took him two weeks to recover sufficiently to attend to his duties as ruler of the Soviet Union. Until then, Molotov was in charge. It was he who delivered the speeches to the citizens of the Soviet Union on Sunday, June 22, 1941, in place of Stalin, who had a heart attack. During the war, Stalin made serious political and strategic mistakes, as a result of which the German troops succeeded in reaching the outskirts of Moscow.

After the war, Stalin refused to recognize the authority of the politbureau and became, quite openly and undisguisedly, a personal dictator. He no longer tolerated any contradiction, and punished severely those who, like Voznessensky, were in disagreement with him. He had, for no reason whatever, brought about the break with Tito, whom he treated with the utmost discourtesy whenever they met, addressing him in the second person singular and calling him by his nickname "Walter." He nearly brought about a break with Mao-Tse-Tung, as a sequel to a report from Beria, who alleged that Mao-Tse-Tung was continuing to correspond privately with Tito, in spite of Stalin's break with him.[1] And he brought about the war in Korea, for he was quite convinced that the U.S.A. would never intervene there, in spite of the fact that the information supplied by the Russian secret service was to the contrary.

Yet although Nikita stressed those errors and misdeeds of Stalin which arose from his anti-Marxist theory of the cult of personality, he tried to show that, by and large, the general line of Stalin's policy had followed that of Lenin.

---

[1] This explains a sentence in the Moscow statement after the arrest of Beria in June 1953, which said: "We shall continue and consolidate our policy of the deepest friendship and of friendly co-operation with China, directed by Mao-Tse-Tung."

"Stalin was compelled to follow it," said Nikita. "And if he was sometimes reluctant to adopt Lenin's principles of collectivization and industrialization, we, the members of the politbureau, did so in our actual governmental activities, often running a serious risk to ourselves. Stalin was so distrustful and suspicious that he considered that everything that was done without his knowledge was treason."

And when discussing the ruthless character of the Big Purge, Nikita had this to say: "Even if the disastrous tactics of the opposition made it necessary to purge them, it was scarcely necessary to exterminate tens of thousands of communists." He further emphasized that the members of the politbureau were not responsible for this course of action, which Stalin had arranged personally with Yezhov.[1]

Stalin, he said, always refused to consult the politbureau on repressive measures against persons arrested by Yezhov, as he maintained that it was the business of the NKVD to adopt these measures against the enemies of the soviet people and State, and that the politbureau had no authority to interfere in such matters.

Nikita concluded his report by pointing out that Stalin had dismissed Molotov from his post as minister of foreign affairs because he wanted to have a "faithful lackey," Vyshinsky, in his stead. He himself had taken over the foreign ministry at the beginning of 1953, and had started by having talks with foreign ambassadors, about which he revealed nothing. In the course of one of these talks with L. Bravo, the ambassador of Peron, Stalin had made a number of promises, in spite of Molotov's protests to the presidium. Molotov was severely reprimanded and threatened with imprisonment.

Nikita's report at the secret session of the twentieth congress was of great interest to the delegates, only a very small num-

[1] Nevertheless, as we have seen in Chapter IX, Nikita had taken part in the Big Purge in the Ukraine.

ber of whom were at all familiar with the last phase of Stalin's rule. A special commission was elected, consisting of Nikita, Zhukov, Molotov, Bulganin and Mikoyan, and presided over by Nikita, to draft a confidential letter to the party cells. This letter was to reproduce the main points of Nikita's report. Another version, simplified and slightly adapted, was intended to be read at meetings of those who were not party members.

As Nikita had anticipated, his secret report had added greatly to his popularity, and enabled them to obtain from the congress a vote in favor of a very important measure: the setting up of the "Bureau of the central committee of the party for the Soviet Federative Socialist Republic of Russia" under the presidency of Nikita. This is the largest federative republic in the Soviet Union, and hitherto was the only one of the sixteen federative republics without a bureau. The central committee of the party for the Soviet Union was supposed to act in the same capacity for the Republic of what is known as Great Russia,[1] comprising the most important part of the Soviet Union. But in actual practice the central committee has never dealt with the republic in question, but has left these matters to the regional committees. Nikita's measure had now readjusted this. His reasons for doing so may be judged from the fact that nearly sixty per cent of soviet industry is located on this territory, and nearly sixty-five per cent of the party members live there. By placing the new special bureau under the charge of persons who are devoted followers of his—Katherine Furtzeva, Kozlov, Aristov and Grishin—Nikita made certain of being supported by the Russian Federative Republic, after having secured the complete fidelity of the Soviet Ukraine, with Kiritchenko as first secre-

---

[1] Great Russia comprises the administrative areas of Orel, Tula, Ryazan, Tambov, Penza, Voronezh, Kursk, Moscow, Vladimir, Yaroslav, Kostroma, Tver, Kaluga, Leningrad, Pskov and Olonetz, together with the northern provinces of Arkhangelsk and Vologda.

tary and Kaltchenko as president of the Council. This was a clever move.

The central committee elections resulted in an increase of representation for the "economists." The committee resulting from the nineteenth party congress in November 1952 had been composed as follows:

> "Apparatchiki".........55 per cent.
> "Economists"..........20 per cent.
> "Military men".........15 per cent.
> Peasants and workers..10 per cent.

It will be noted that peasants and workers, toiling in fields and factories, had accounted for only ten per cent of the members of the central committee of the party "of the dictatorship of the workers," whereas the three categories of bureaucrats had totalled ninety per cent between them. In Nikita's new central committee, the outcome of the twentieth congress, the total percentage of bureaucrats remained the same, but it was split up differently:

> "Apparatchiki".........45 per cent.
> "Economists"..........25 per cent.
> "Military men".........20 per cent.
> Peasants and workers.10 per cent.

Thus, the party bureaucrats formed only forty-five per cent of the new central committee. They no longer had an absolute majority, and would not, as before be able to constitute, by themselves, a solid opposition. Nevertheless, Nikita's "apparatchiki" still remained the most important faction among the soviet bureaucrats, and they could easily dominate the others, by support from the peasants and workers. This explains Nikita's new maneuver. He was currying favor with the masses, improving their standard of living, attending to their general welfare, increasing their wages. In this way he wanted to give the masses the impression that the Soviet

Union was evolving from a bureaucratic state to a state in which "popular justice," a Russian fetish, would be paramount.

Nikita, a peasant-worker, a self-taught man who had become a statesman, a left-wing socialist transmogrified into a "hundred per cent Leninist bolshevik," was attracted by the idea of a State in which "popular justice" would be paramount —far more so than men like Malenkov or Bulganin. A large number of the "military men," themselves of popular origin, undoubtedly approved of the new party line, the essential feature of which was Nikita's fixed determination to become a "popular ataman"[1] of the masses. He had behind him a long apprenticeship in the bureaucratic mechanism of the Soviet Union. He was familiar with all the defects of this mechanism, which he manipulated with great skill.

The new presidium of the central committee, as constituted by him, contained eleven members: Kaganovitch, Bulganin, Voroshilov, Mikoyan, Saburov, Pervukin, Molotov, Kisitchenko and, of course, himself, together with six deputy-members: Shvernik, Breynev, Mukhittidinov, Shepilov, Zhukov and Furtzeva.

In this presidium Nikita had a marginal majority sufficient to impose his personal bias upon the home and foreign policy of the Soviet Union. While, as regards home policy, Nikita had moved sharply towards "democratization by the masses for the masses," the foreign policy of his country was still handicapped by the Stalin heritage.

Nikita Khrushchev's report to the twentieth congress brought world renown to a man who was scarcely known outside Russia.

[1] The word "ataman" is of Turkoman origin. It has found its way into Russian and Ukrainian, but not with the same shade of meaning. In Russian it implies a robber chieftain, an outlaw, sometimes a brigand or rebel. In Ukrainian it has come to mean a leader or chief, elected by the Cossacks in a democratic manner.

The Khrushchev Report was a historical event of great importance; it bridged two eras. It also added the wily Ukrainian's name to the pages of history.

Stalin had bequeathed a totalitarian regime to his heirs. The Khrushchev Report marked the beginning of an irreversible process in the politics of the U.S.S.R. This was the process of democratization.

We have already noted that Khrushchev was influenced to some degree by those who, like Mikoyan, asked for the outright condemnation of Stalin's regime and policies. Freed at last from the yoke of tyranny and suspicion, the reigning Soviet bureaucracy envisioned a veritable Magna Charta of freedoms as a guarantee against a repetition of the Stalinists' errors that had cost thousands of officials their lives.

Nikita Khrushchev pledged these freedoms in his report. He told how Stalin liquidated high-ranking officials and how he intended to bring about the demise of such members of the Politbureau as Kaganovitch, Mikoyan, Voroshilov and Molotov following Vosnessensky's execution on account of his part in the Leningrad affair.

But Khrushchev failed to breathe a word about the liquidation of hundreds of thousands of peasants during Stalin's attempt to bring about collectivization by force. He was nevertheless familiar with statistics drawn up by Soviet officials: about 5,000,000 peasant families were uprooted during the attempt to collectivize them. Even if we allow for the resettlement of some of these families, we are still unable to account for several hundred thousand victims of Stalin's brutal methods.

Khrushchev had very good reasons for saying nothing about the collectivization attempt in his report. The purportedly socialistic and collectivized rural areas had fallen into the same pattern as every other phase of life in the U.S.S.R. They had their profiteers and upper-caste Kolkhozians, so dubbed by Stalin in recognition of their services; these privileged few were the new "socialist kulaks." Nikita dared not attack them. He was once forced to acknowledge their influence and admit that "the de-Stalinization of the country has encountered serious difficulties."

These preliminary remarks are designed to stress the importance of the Khrushchev Report. Its immediate aim was to transform the Soviet bureaucracy into a privileged class and at the same time to give the other classes reason to hope that some kind of socialist law would slowly but surely better their lives.

Nikita had to move cautiously: Stalin's name might be used by disgruntled followers, especially in the Caucasus, where the execution of Beria and his accomplices had caused considerable unrest; on March 7, 1956, riots had broken out in Georgia and in Baku. A regional member of the Presidium of the Central Committee of the Russian Communist Party, Mir Baghirov, a Tartar from Azerbaidjan, had had a hand in it. Baghirov had been excluded from the Presidium after Beria's arrest but had not otherwise been bothered for some time. He had gone to Baku with other Georgian or Azerbaidjan Berianists to direct a clandestine campaign against Khrushchev and the new co-operative leadership. He was arrested after the riots in the Caucasus and tried before the Military College in April 1956; he was condemned to death. His execution, which took place during the London visit of "K-B," was kept secret for a month.

Baghirov was accused of having been a backwoods outlaw—in 1917! The accusation may well have been true, for half of the Caucasian revolutionaries of that time had some dealings with mountaineers who lived outside the reach of law.

Beria and his accomplices, as well as Baghirov, were condemned and executed according to the Law of December 1,

1934, which allowed Stalin to execute almost every one of Lenin's supporters. The law allows the Military College to mete out the death penalty to *anyone, without the slightest proof of guilt, in time of peace!* It even provides for judging the accused *in their absence* (we now know that Beria was absent during his trial and that the transcripts were falsified as freely as the official records of Ulrich,[1] the celebrated falsifier who headed the Military College during Stalin's time). Nikita had promised repeatedly that the "abject law of December, 1934" would be abrogated. But the law still exists, and it is rumored in Moscow that the military authorities opposed its annulment.

It is obvious that the Law of December 1, 1934, is held like the sword of Damocles over the head of anyone who might wish to rise up against the new leaders of the U.S.S.R., and thus gives the upper hand to the military.

The Khrushchev Report was never intended for the press. A circular was sent out to all cells by the central committee of the party. This circular contained few of the scabrous details of the original speech. The version sent to other communist parties was further expurgated, but provoked the world-wide sensation headlined as "Khrushchev's Secret Report."

[1] He committed suicide after Stalin's death.

XX

TRIPS TO WARSAW AND LONDON

On March 12, 1956, Nikita went to Warsaw, where he attended the funeral services of Boleslaw Bierut, the First Secretary of the United Polish Workers Party, and witnessed the election of his successor, Ochab.

A foreign diplomat, the representative of a neutral Asiatic member of the Commonwealth, used this opportunity to talk to Khrushchev about the Report during his visit. The American press had reported on it at length and had omitted no irrational detail. Dozens of members had fainted during Khrushchev's address to the Congress, it was said. Fantastic plans were attributed to Nikita.

"Do you know, Mr. Khrushchev," asked the diplomat, "that they are spreading fantastic rumors about your report?"

"There is also a Russian proverb that says 'Never trust a rumor,' " replied Nikita.

"But why not publish your report in full?"

"You should never wash dirty linen in front of strangers. You should wash it in the family."

154

"But you are not dealing with linen. You are dealing with human lives!"

Khrushchev looked coldly at the diplomat and said:

"I am no diplomat, but I know that for you diplomats, the true value of human lives in politics was explained by Macchiavelli. Have you read him?"

"Everyone has read *The Prince*."

"I am not speaking of *The Prince*, Mr. Diplomat. I am speaking of Macchiavelli's famous *Memoir* for diplomats."[1]

The diplomat admitted that he had never read the *Memoir*. "I have read extracts from it," said Nikita, "in a book by Vladimir Potemkins, our diplomat-historian. In Leningrad there is a very rare copy of Macchiavelli's book; it contains a marginal note written by Macchiavelli himself; according to that note:

" '. . . human life has only negative value so far as the diplomat is concerned, for every man whom he meets along his road is *an obstacle to be surmounted*.' "

The Asiatic diplomat realized that Nikita was well versed in diplomacy.

"That's how it is," Nikita said. Then he continued: "I have to go to London with Bulganin. British newspapers are afraid that I shall conduct myself badly in the presence of the queen because I am coarse and ill-bred. What they really mean is that I am an old man who was once a swineherd. I aim to show that Soviet statesmen are second to none . . . In his *Memoir*, Macchiavelli outlined in detail the protocol to be observed. . . . You know, Mr. Diplomat, that Macchiavelli was sent to France as an envoy near the end of the fifteenth century. In his book he even set down a 'list of tips to be distributed!' This is what he said:

" '. . . to outside doormen, give one ducat; to the wardrobe attendant, four ducats; to trumpeters, *nothing!* As for gifts

[1] He meant the future Ambassador's *Memento*.

to the Court, the more generous you are, the better it is . . . .' "

Nikita laughed heartily and finished by saying:

"You, Sir, represent a member of the Commonwealth. If you have the opportunity, please let it be known in London that the former swineherd will conduct himself like a perfect gentleman at the royal reception."

Nikita Khrushchev kept his word. He did not make a single diplomatic blunder during his visit to London in April, 1956; the gifts distributed during the visit were made in accordance with Nicholas Macchiavelli's advice. Blunders were rather on the side of Britain: Lionel Crabb, the hapless frogman, died under the keel of the Orjonikidze, the cruiser that had brought "K-B" to London, during an attempt at underwater espionage. On that occasion Nikita conducted himself with perfect discretion. He did not even take advantage of the debates staged in the House of Commons by the Laborites, who attacked Sir Anthony Eden on account of the lack of courtesy shown by the British information services.

It is quite possible that Nikita Khrushchev, who was a diligent reader of Macchiavelli, had also read his *Rittrati delle cose di Francia*. This work recounts the celebrated diplomat-writer-dramatist's travels through France. In it Macchiavelli stated that "the necessity of acquainting oneself with a country and its envoys takes place first; the statesman uses every possible means to accomplish this end. . . ."

XXI

TALKS WITH TITO

The trip to London, as well as the arrival of Millet and Pineau in Moscow on May 15, was but a necessary intermission during the lengthy conferences with Tito, which had been initiated by "K-B" in 1955 and prolonged by Anastasia Mikoyan, who had gone to Yugoslavia several times in 1955 and 1956.

Nikita played his ace: *reconciliation with Belgrade*. He understood clearly that his soft approach and the de-Stalinization practiced by the U.S.S.R. would arouse much controversy in the satellite countries. He wanted to avoid having criticism directed at the U.S.S.R. The external security of Russia was at stake; the members of the General Staff of the U.S.S.R. repeatedly warned the First Secretary of the Central Committee of the Communist Party.

Their fears were well founded. In case of a schism among the satellite countries, the security of the U.S.S.R. would have been gravely affected. A military newspaper, the

Voienny Viestnika, had published an interesting article on the subject:

"The problems of future wars will not be the same as the problems of World War II. Future wars will be push-button affairs. We must have radar stations set up hundreds of miles beyond our borders to warn us against enemy missiles fifteen or twenty minutes in advance of their arrival."

And the newspaper concluded:

"Some members of the Warsaw pact, such as Albania and *Hungary,* are especially important as watch-towers, for radar stations vital to the security of the U.S.S.R. can be installed in these countries."

Tito arrived during the early part of June, 1956. Madam Jovanka Broz went with him.

"I want the people of the U.S.S.R. to see the most beautiful specimen of feminine beauty among the Yugoslavs," Nikita had said.

Tito's reception in the capital of the U.S.S.R. was regal. A crowd of about 500,000 men and women filled the streets and public squares of Moscow. Their shouts and cheers continued. Tito was so touched by the demonstration that he wept. Seated beside "B-K" and Voroshilov, he answered the cheering crowd. Madam Jovanka Broz was covered with flowers. For Tito this was a personal triumph. As a former party worker, he had held a subordinate position in the Komintern and was accustomed to occupy a room in a second-rate Moscow hotel, the Lux. Then a relatively obscure man, he was nicknamed Walter; few of the party leaders knew him by his real name (Stalin did not learn it until 1942 and continued even after that to address him, during Tito's visit to Moscow in 1946, as Walter). His triumph was complete.

The reception was enough to turn the "heretical" Marshal's head. His appearance in the Soviet Capital made him the winner of his quarrel with Stalin. On the day that Tito arrived, Nikita presented him with a royal gift: the dismissal of Molotov from his post as Minister of Foreign Affairs. This was the man who had signed, along with Stalin, the letter marking the break with Tito and threatening him with total liquidation.

Nikita was putting his cards on the table: definitive, complete reconciliation with the U.S.S.R.; Belgrade's entrance into the socialist camp on her own terms of complete independence; and generous aid from the U.S.S.R. to Yugoslavia.

Tito had no part in the Western bloc. As an outspoken opponent of blocs in general, he recommended their liquidation. Nikita freely accepted the liquidation of NATO and the Warsaw Pact *in principle*, but he invited the Marshal from Belgrade to make a pretense of showing his preference for the U.S.S.R., the leader of the socialist camp, in exchange for economic, financial and political compensations. Political compensations included *the progressive emancipation of the satellite countries*. This was to assure Tito that the U.S.S.R. had no aggressive intentions against the satellites. It was his guarantee that the complete independence of Yugoslavia would be respected to the letter in the future.

Such was the real meaning of the Big Play that Nikita inaugurated in Belgrade and continued in Moscow. His spokesman, Major General Kornyenko, stated in his article that Soviet occupation of satellite countries was no longer of any military value so long as these countries remained inside the Soviet zone of influence and kept their Popular Front governments in power. If Yugoslavia came back into the fold, satellite regimes could be liberalized without endangering the U.S.S.R.

In other words, Nikita's proposal was this: as soon as you come back into our camp, the liberation of the satellite countries will be completed. The ground work was laid for new projects—Danube Federation, Mid-European Alliance, etc.—

which would usher in a new era of collaboration "following the economic and political pattern of the U.S.S.R."

Tito's Yugoslavia could become the nucleus of a new alignment of powers. . . .

Thus the negotiations between Tito and "K-B" had an auspicious beginning. The crowd continued to applaud Tito's address. The Moscow crowd looked upon this occasion as something more than the return of a Yugoslav nationalist to the Communist fold; they looked upon Tito as the son of a Slavic nation which had had close ties with Russia for a long time. In 1875 Russian volunteers led by General Cherniaieff had come to Serbia to direct the revolt against the Turks. In the seventeenth century, Yuri Krijanitch left Croatia to become the leader of the first pan-Slav movement. They remembered, too, the beautiful and distant landscapes of Dalmatia, Illyria, and Montenegro; their greatest national poet, Pushkin, had popularized their folklore.

Though Marshal Tito had plenty of trumps in his hand, "K" had indicated from the beginning the limitations which he wanted to place on the negotiations:

"We wipe out the past. We admit that Yugoslavia is a socialist country even though you renounced our methods for the edification of socialism. You took the risk of adopting other methods and succeeded. I congratulate you, Comrade Tito! But as for the other people's democracies, let them continue to work toward socialism through the methods that they have adopted. Do not try to impose on them your own example of Yugoslav methods."

Khrushchev was willing to allow Yugoslavia to continue her own "national communism" methods but refused to allow other countries in the Soviet zone to follow her example. He was willing to allow nothing more than the liberalization of their own regimes: the disappearance of the all-powerful secret police, the cessation of rule by fear and a few "liberal" reforms which would bring about some superficial changes in these countries.

But Nikita had committed a psychological blunder that was to have important consequences. He had unwittingly placed a halo on the great chieftain of heresy by the triumphal reception which he had arranged for him. For Nikita had organized the welcome that culminated in the delirious demonstration that marked the entry of the Marshal from Belgrade into the capital of the U.S.S.R. Nikita had given Tito impressive *moral* authority in the eyes of the peoples of the satellite countries. All the disgruntled people of these countries—all those who wanted to shake off the yoke of the U.S.S.R. for nationalist or social reasons—now had a pretext: Stalin was guilty! This was the man who had personified uninterrupted terror and national humiliation for the satellite countries for eight long years.

Tito had placed a crown on Lenin's tomb, but had avoided Stalin's tomb. His gesture added to the confusion that reigned throughout the satellites as well as in Moscow.

A foreign diplomat who understood Russian told of a conversation which he overheard in Red Square:

"You know," said one Russian to another, "Tito said that Stalin was a dirty scoundrel and that he would not put a wreath on his grave."

His interlocutor replied: "They even say that Tito spit whenever he mentioned Stalin!"

During the initial negotiations between Tito and Khrushchev, the State Department managed to accomplish a deft maneuver. For once Mr. Dulles, thanks to his brother Allen, the head of the C.I.A., took top honors.

On June 4, 1956, right in the middle of Tito's stay in Moscow, the State Department published the text of Khrushchev's speech of February 25, 1956, delivered before the twentieth congress of the Russian communist party.

After the sensational accounts of the newspapers, the whole world was finally able to read a document that represented a fairly authentic version of Nikita Khrushchev's secret report.

And the version released by the State Department does seem fairly authentic. There is reason to suppose that the report, which was probably changed and inflated somewhat during the course of its transmission, was picturesque enough in its original form.

That some passages of the released version are inaccurate is suggested by the wording. Near the end of the version published by the United Press, Mr. Khrushchev is reported to have told how Stalin had transcripts of the famous trial of the Soviet doctors sent *to the members of the Politbureau.* It is common knowledge, and this information has appeared in print, that the scandal did not break until December, 1952. The Politbureau had already been dissolved by the decision of the nineteenth pan-Russian congress of the communist party, which took place during the first part of October, 1952, two months before the scandal involving the doctors. The Politbureau had been replaced by the Presidium of the Central Committee, and Stalin must have sent the transcripts to its members. It seems certain that this mistake could not have originated with Khrushchev. It was added during the transmission of the text. There are other mistakes concerning the names of persons unjustly accused by Stalin. Among them is a certain Alexis Sniegoff, who was secretary of the central committee of the party of Winnitza and Poltova as well as an official of the central committee of the Ukrainian communist party of Kharkov, where he was arrested. In the version edited by the State Department, Sniegoff is cited as an official of the local committee of the Caucasus; there he was a so-called witness to the settling of accounts between Beria and a man called Lavrentiev, who was the local secretary in

Georgia. It should also be noted that the story of a man called Kedrov, supposedly condemned to death by Beria under the pretext that he was a former agitator for the Ochrana, is pure invention. To be sure, there was once a man named Kedrov who held an official position in the N.K.V.D.; he had once been a student in the school of medicine and had the title of doctor. He was notoriously unbalanced and sadistic. As a result of a special decision of the N.K.V.D. (then the O.G.P.U.), Kedrov was shot in 1926. Though Beria was a high official of the O.G.P.U. of Tiflis at that time, he was not the one responsible for Kedrov's execution.

There is also a flagrant error with respect to Kossior. There were three brothers named Kossior, all of whom were high officials in the Russian communist party. One of the three brothers, Vladimir, was shot by the N.K.V.D. The other two, one of whom was Stanislas, the ex-secretary of the central committee of the Ukraine, committed suicide in their prison cells in Yakutsk.[1] The State Department version says that Stanislas was shot. Khrushchev could scarcely have been responsible for this mistake. There are a number of editorial inaccuracies concerning the text of Lenin's testament. For example, one sentence added by Lenin in his characterization of Bukharin and Piatakov, is missing in its entirety; the sentence points out that Bukharin and Piatakov, among all the party leaders, are the most capable of administering the country. *The same mistake* appeared in 1934 in a Trotskyite newspaper published abroad. The State Department version obviously borrowed from the opposition newspaper edited by Trotskyites. Numerous passages in Lenin's letter to Stalin also show signs of editorial tampering.

Just why Nikita Khrushchev never saw fit to deny the "dressed-up" text of his report is not clear.

Another circumstance arouses suspicion: Khrushchev's ac-

[1] They were transferred there from Moscow.

count of Stalin' mistakes in external politics was largely deleted. Is its omission due to the services affiliated to the State Department or to the ill-will of a Party official—a Stalinist who wanted to deal Nikita a low blow by divulging his secret report to the Americans? Or is the omission due to the opposition?

All the intrigues practiced now by the Polish Stalinists in an effort to stack the deck against their enemy Gomulka suggest that the Stalinists of Moscow were quite capable of playing the same trick on Khrushchev, especially on the day following the dismissal of their chieftain, Molotov.

In any event, the publication of the secret report immediately disrupted the negotiations between Khrushchev and Tito. The Georgian suffered international defamation. Everybody talked about his mistakes and his crimes. The rehabilitation of all his victims was sought. Trotsky's widow even sent a telegram to Khrushchev. The heretical Tito became an international hero who, like St. George, had no hesitancy in combatting a new dragon which was the most dangerous dragon ever swallowed by the international communist movement: Joseph Stalin, the Borgia of world communism. No longer was it possible for Tito, now a candidate for the post of Stalin's ideological successor, to accept Khrushchev's modest Belgrade proposal: to grant complete autonomy within the communist movement to Yugoslavia without granting the same independence to the Soviet satellites.

Khrushchev went on a trip through the U.S.S.R. with Tito in order to be able to negotiate without interferences and beyond the reach of any member of the Politbureau. He wanted to persuade the Marshal from Belgrade to accept a compromise that would be acceptable to the Presidium of the Central Committee. Tito was intractable.

Tito would not concede that communist countries should

be forced to acknowledge the supremacy of the U.S.S.R. He felt that this would bring about a resurgence of Russian Imperialism. "Lenin said that two dangers confronted the international communist movement: the danger of imperialistic chauvinism and the danger of national movements among small nations. He believed that the first danger was more serious than the second."

Nikita could only reply: "Lenin said many things, but he finally acknowledged the necessity of annexing Georgia in February, 1921, after having opposed our army's invasion of that country."

In 1956 the situation was no longer the same as it was when Lenin expounded his dogma in 1921–1923: the U.S.S.R. had become the strongest socialist power in the world and rivaled the U.S.A. Only their relative equality in resources and atomic arms prevented a generalized military conflict. Each bloc tried to whittle away at the other, but neither wanted to risk another world war. From Khrushchev's viewpoint, without Russian aid, the satellite countries would be quickly overrun by the U.S.A. Tito might have countered by pointing out that Yugoslavia had not been swallowed up, and that he was as firmly in control of his country as the leaders of the U.S.S.R. were of theirs.

Tito did not wish to acknowledge that Khrushchev was right and vice versa. It was obvious that the visit was not going to produce the positive results that Nikita had hoped for.

But the First Secretary of the Central Committee of the Russian Communist Party could not make an outright admission of his failure. His flirtation with Tito and especially his humiliating treatment of Molotov had caused a stir in the Presidium. Bulganin still stood firmly behind his friend Nikita. The military leaders, headed by Zhukov, also supported him. Marshal Moskalenko, who was called the Praetorian Marshal, had Moscow in firm control. The troops in the capital were reliable. But Khrushchev understood also that the military leaders would desert him the moment his political course endangered the security of the U.S.S.R., with respect to either Tito or the satellite countries. The old-line Stalinists were already talking about his disgrace and even about his arrest. His language and excessive use of alcohol were mentioned. He needed to make an open and unequivocal statement of his loyalty to the Party and his determination to deal firmly with the Russian satellites.

That is what he did. When he visited Stalingrad with Tito, Khrushchev delivered a resounding speech[1] before several thousand workers:

"We have brought about many changes. We have bettered the lives of workers. We are on the verge of reaping a harvest such as the U.S.S.R. has never before known. From fifteen to eighteen million tons of surplus wheat will go into our storage-bins and silos. No one will ever go hungry in the U.S.S.R. No one. I stake my life on it. Soon we shall be rich and prosperous enough to help our brothers and comrades in the people's democracies. Do you agree?"

"We agree," shouted the crowd assembled before Khrushchev and Tito.

"We have with us Comrade Tito, the glorious leader of the Yugoslav people," Khrushchev continued. "He has come to our country to observe our progress. Last year I went to Belgrade to visit him and to see what had been accomplished there. Much progress has been made. But whatever progress they have made is the result of your victory over the Nazis at Stalingrad. Without your military victory and our victory in establishing socialism, Yugoslavia could not have succeeded in consolidating and building up her economy."

"Bravo!" shouted the crowd.

[1] Reported in the Stalingrad newspaper.

At that moment Tito indicated that he wished to speak. Khrushchev put him off:

"Just a moment, Comrade Tito. I am going to finish in five minutes—I say that life will be easier, more enjoyable for everyone. But I also say that our party has decided to exercise tight control in order to insure that our perfidious enemies will not wreck the Soviet state. And I say to you—I, Nikita Khrushchev, former swineherd and worker from Donetz—that I would rather have my arms and legs cut off than live in a state not governed by the communist party. Never, never would I consent to dig a grave for the U.S.S.R. and our allies, the other people's democracies."

After he had spoken these words on the soil of Stalingrad, Khrushchev turned toward Tito.

Tito understood. But he was in no mood to give in. He left the U.S.S.R. after having signed an ambiguous declaration that could be interpreted in either of two ways by each party to the discussion: the U.S.S.R. and Yugoslavia.

On the surface, everything seemed to be calm and orderly, but underneath were hidden the seeds of an imminent storm.

The Poznan uprising was the first outward sign of what was to follow.

XXII

FAREWELL PARTY

The aura of official friendship that marked the end of Marshal Tito's visit to Moscow could be interpreted in one way by the Russians and in another by the Yugoslavs.

Before allowing his guest to depart, Nikita Khrushchev wanted to offer an intimate reception in his honor. He invited no journalists and no ranking Soviet officials except for a few select members of the Presidium of the Central Committee of the communist party, the Presidium of the Supreme Soviet and the government of the Soviet Union.

About one hundred people assembled on the former estate of Prince Sheremetiev, not far from Moscow. The Prince was the favorite of Peter the Great and served as his ambassador. The Soviet dignitaries brought their wives along to keep Madam Jovanka Broz company.[1]

Prince Sheremetiev's estate is known for its huge pond on which Peter the Great learned to sail in his youth. It was near this pond that the first Emperor of Modern Russia be-

[1] Reported by the Yugoslav press.

came acquainted with Menchikoff, a merchant whom he subsequently raised to the highest post in the Russian government (one of his descendants is now the Soviet ambassador to New Delhi).

It was a beautiful evening in June, 1956. Khrushchev, Tito, Bulganin, Mikoyan, Voroshilov, Shepilov and a small group of intimates left the ladies and crossed the pond on a ferry. They reached a small artificial island with a lovers' cave that had once been the trysting place of noble Russian suitors. Freshly painted benches had been placed in the cave which was dimly lighted by Chinese lanterns. Everything was calm and peaceful. No one would have guessed that the words exchanged in the secluded cave would be the prologue to events that would have world-wide repercussions.

Molotov was absent. He had excused himself, saying that he was indisposed. "A diplomat's disease," Nikita remarked as he passed the excuse on to Tito. Then he added:

"We have a Russian proverb that says, 'Tell me who your associates are, and I'll tell you who you are.' Comrade Molotov has been in the diplomatic service too long. He has developed bad habits."

Tito was worried. He was well aware of the gravity of the stalemate reached in the negotiations that brought him to the capital of the U.S.S.R. He was probably wondering what effect the stalemate would have on international relations and on relations between Moscow and Belgrade. Their new friendship was still precarious.

"Comrade Tito is not in good form today," said Nikita with a hearty laugh. "Anastasia Ivanovich,[1] bring your guitar."

Mikoyan appeared with his historic guitar.[2]

[1] Mikoyan.
[2] Mikoyan had used the same guitar many times to calm the outbursts of an aging and tyrannical Stalin.

"Play the Gulindzhan," said Nikita.

Mikoyan's tenor voice was heard:

> ". . . . If you do not love me,
> My life is not worthwhile;
> I shall go to the river
> And drown myself. . . ."

"Bravo," shouted Nikita, and half-banteringly, half-seriously, he addressed the group:

"Listen carefully to this song. It is quite appropriate. If our dear guest refuses to love me, I, Nikita Khrushchev, will drown myself in this pond."

Everyone laughed at his joke. Having broken the ice, Nikita continued:

"This island is not like the others. It has a history, and I am speaking of Soviet history. When Lenin had begun to recover somewhat from his illness, before his second attack, he was brought to the Sheremetiev estate to hunt one day. He was as happy as a child when he succeeded in killing a crow."

Mikoyan, who was listening disinterestedly to Nikita, was obviously annoyed:

"Listen, Nikita. Zinoviev was responsible for that story. I think he made the whole thing up."

"That's possible. I never liked Zinoviev, though I think there was no real reason for shooting him. But the story is true. Lashevitch, who was also present, confirmed it."

A full red moon emerged from behind a cloud. Putting his hand on Tito's shoulder, Nikita continued:

"I am accused of sentimentality. All of us Ukrainians are a little sentimental. The moon brings out our feelings. I shall never forget a moonlit night on the island of Brioni."

Tito smiled. He had every reason to remember a nocturnal bath taken by Nikita at Brioni.

"Finally, to come back to my story, Ilich had told Zinoviev:

'I should like to come back here again with all the members of the Politburo, including Trotsky and Stalin, and have them take an oath here, in the cave—an oath before the workers and peasants of our country, an oath that would be sealed by. . . .' "

Nikita became silent, then continued:

"A solemn oath to avoid any fratricidal shedding of blood!"

"Finally," Mikoyan added, "you are proposing to Comrade Tito an eternal and a solemn military non-aggression pact, aren't you? Don't you wish to limit military actions in the future to the battle of circulars and speeches?"

"I propose that we swear to remain comrades no matter what happens!"

"Good," said Mikoyan. "If you insist, I'll administer the oath to both you and Comrade Tito. I studied theology at the seminary of Tiflis."

Smiling, Mikoyan strummed the "Gulindzhan" on his historic guitar. Nikita's face suddenly became serious:

"There are clouds on the horizon."

A group gathered around Nikita. They looked at him, somewhat surprised. What did the First Secretary of the Communist Party mean by the words "clouds on the horizon"?

Nikita started to address the guests:

"At Belgrade and Brioni, Marshal Tito and I laid the groundwork for a new era. I believe firmly in the possibility of a socialist transformation of the world on the basis of peaceful co-existence. . . . Our friendship with Comrade Tito is proof of success. I promise to make every effort to ensure that this friendship will never die."

Taking Tito by the arm, he led him away, followed by the other guests.

The reception held in Prince Sheremetiev's summer palace ended rather early in the evening.

XXIII

UNREST IN POLAND

Nikita's apprehensions were not groundless. One week after the reception at Sheremetiev Palace, the Soviet ambassador to Warsaw, Ponomarenko, arrived in Moscow. He brought with him a detailed report made by Colonel Molotchkov, a security officer who served as liaison agent between the Russians and the Polish security police.

The report indicated that discontent was spreading among the workers and that the peasants were ready to start an open revolt against the collective farms.

Ponomarenko went to see Khrushchev. The two men were not on good terms: during Stalin's time, Ponomarenko, then the secretary general of the communist party of Byelorussia, was jealous of Khrushchev because of his meteoric rise. After Stalin's death Ponomarenko, then a member of the Presidium, had surreptitiously supported Beria against "K-B." But he was smart enough to drop his ally in time, with the result that his punishment was limited to the loss of his seat on the Presidium of the Central Committee of the party.

He was sent to Central Asia as secretary of the local committee of the communist party of Kazakhstan. After he had spent some time there, he was sent to Warsaw as Ambassador.

In his report, Ponomarenko brought proof that Oshab was carrying on secret correspondence with Tito.

Both Polish and Yugoslav newspapers published numerous items concerning this troubled period. It was said that a violent quarrel had broken out between the First Secretary of the Central Committee and the Ambassador to Warsaw. Ponomarenko forced the recall of Oshab and criticized Nikita for having chosen him to replace Bierut. It was also said that Khrushchev was in firm control and that he had been able to impose his viewpoint during a session of the Presidium of the Central Committee devoted to Ponomarenko's report. The newspapers spoke of Mr. Molotov's hurt pride, of his satisfaction over his quick revenge, and of his open accusations against Tito; he was said to have accused Tito of trying to plot with the satellite countries and draw them away from the U.S.S.R. Press reports also mentioned Marshal Zhukov's stand in his stubborn defense of Nikita. It was even thought that Marshal Zhukov used the Potsdam Agreement, which gave the U.S.S.R. the right to station troops in Poland in order to guarantee lines of communication between Moscow and Germany, to support his stand. For the first time, a new idea was introduced into the discussion: the Warsaw Pact could be dissolved and the Soviet occupation of the satellite countries ended if NATO could be dissolved simultaneously and the American troops withdrawn from the soil of Western Europe.

A Scandinavian newspaper published an extremely interesting report concerning one of Khrushchev's pronouncements. Khrushchev was said to have spoken of the former

Soviet base at Porkhala and "of the right of the Soviet Union to use lines of communication across Finland, but without including this country among the bloc of people's democracies." The same newspaper also reported that Khrushchev's attitude could never be shared by the Molotov group.

Finally Mr. Ben, Warsaw correspondent for the French newspaper *World,* while confirming Marshal Zhukov's benevolent attitude towards Poland, also reported that the Polish rulers were frankly hostile to Mikoyan's soft approach. There was talk of a statement that irritated even the Polophiles in the Kremlin. The statement, apparently originated by one of the Polish leaders, was this: "Poland is like Jesus Christ; it was crucified between two thieves, Russia and Germany."

Multiple and endless conversations took place among the leaders of the Kremlin at this time. The conversations were sometimes continued in the corridors. Once a diplomat from a neutral country saw Mikoyan and Khrushchev seated on a bench. Mikoyan spoke heatedly in true Caucasian fashion. Nikita listened attentively to Mikoyan. His lips parted sometimes as if he wished to answer him, but he said nothing. His features hardened. Perhaps he would have liked to answer Mikoyan, an Armenian, and tell him that he, Nikita the Ukrainian, had stronger reasons to distrust a Pole than he; for he was the son of a people who had suffered an uninterrupted series of wars and massacres at the hands of the Poles for four long centuries; he was the descendant of Ukrainian peasants who had been forced to leave the Poland of Potoski and Radzivill to escape the yoke of humiliation. He, too, could have raised his voice and called for the measures which Ponomarenko sought. It would be easy to send thirty or forty more divisions to Poland and to cover the country with a network of Russian troops so thick that no open revolt could ever be attempted. He could give full authority to Koniev who needed only Nikita's consent to play the role of Marshal Paskievitch amid the ruins of Warsaw. And repeat the ignoble act of the barbaric marshal who announced to Czar Nicholas I, another barbarian, that "order reigns in Warsaw." Nikita felt that the Presidium awaited only a word from him to initiate the preventive measures to be taken.

According to articles that appeared in the press, Ponomarenko's report to the Presidium had this outcome: the Soviet Ambassador to Warsaw was to keep close watch over the situation and to communicate to the Kremlin daily the slightest sign or indication of trouble. According to press accounts, Marshal Koniev was summoned to Moscow on June 28, and General Serov[1] was sent on a confidential mission to Poland.

On June 28, 1956, the Poznan revolt broke out.

A new discussion, in which Koniev took part, was held in the Presidium. Nikita felt that his colleagues were drawing further and further away from him. Even Bulganin frequently abstained during routine votes, as if he were preparing to leave his "side-kick" to his disgruntled opponents.

Following a stormy discussion in the Presidium, it was decided to send confidential circulars to all communist parties in the satellite countries immediately, in order to put them on guard against Tito, the "crypto-socialist" and "incorrigible deviationist."

But the postscript added by Nikita said: "We sincerely hope that Comrade Tito, despite his defects, will remain the friend of the U.S.S.R. Since he is quick-tempered by nature, this letter might needlessly upset him."[2]

"K" wanted to remain faithful to the oath taken in Prince Sheremetiev's cave.

But he had to stand up against those members of the Presidium who wanted to send Molotov and Malenkov to the eighth

---

1 Head of the Committee for Internal Security.
2 Reported by the American press.

plenary session of the Unified Polish Workers Party to take the party in hand.

Nikita volunteered his refusal (even though, as First Secretary of the Central Committee, it was his duty to go). He nominated Bulganin and added the name of Marshal Zhukov. He suggested that they be sent on July 21.

The situation was delicate. The faithful support of Marshal Zhukov convinced Nikita that he would be able to surmount all difficulties. The great, silent army was with him, for Zhukov was the whole army. And perhaps the country was with him, too. His popularity in the U.S.S.R. continued to grow. Among all the members of the Presidium, he alone was undiscussed and above discussion; he alone enjoyed undisputed power.

Khrushchev realized that the only way of keeping a firm grip on Poland, without using violence, was through a strong Polish government which would collaborate in good faith with the U.S.S.R. within the framework of the Warsaw Pact.

Still, he was due to be disillusioned. His disillusionment did not stem from the "enemies of the working classes" but from the members of the Politburo of Poland. During his trip with Zhukov, "B" made speeches about the "counter-revolution" unleashed by the Poznan uprising; a report, written by Ponamarenko, arrived from Warsaw and, almost simultaneously, a letter from an annoyed Tito.

The Politbureau of the Unified Polish Workers Party had sent Khrushchev's secret letter to Tito.

According to the sense of duty among "brother" communist parties of different countries, Khrushchev's act constituted treason. But it was too late to react. It was near the end of July, 1956. The eighth plenary session of the Central Committee of the Polish Communist Party had ended. Gomulka had been reintegrated into the party. Marshal Koniev had taken every measure necessary for the establishment of maximum security: seven fresh divisions had arrived to take up quarters around the Polish capital.

The strong support of Marshal Zhukov and the army allowed Khrushchev to steer past a dangerous reef and lie at anchor pending a change in the situation. But the end of July had brought something unexpected; this time the army gave Nikita his cue: The Suez affair erupted with Nasser's nationalization of the canal.

minister of Pravda, could disclaim had seemed to exist at a minimum around the VIth Congress.

Also the approach of Chairest Khrushchev and the floor of power in an ever-increasing or declining and honesty that power was increasingly understood that the end of July in all internal something that appears to inform time since Stalin's death news the news that seemed in all future position around.

XXIV

FROM SUEZ TO JAKHARTA

The official publication of the General Staff of the U.S.S.R. had alluded to certain "important meetings and conferences affecting national security."

Some of the meetings alluded to were undoubtedly military in nature. But one meeting of the Presidium was of extraordinary importance.

The Near East question was broached. This question had caused a number of wars, including the Crimean, during Russia's history. A French diplomat called it the question "that smelled of powder for a thousand leagues around."

It will be recalled that Shepilov's policy of militant anticolonialism was supposed to win for the U.S.S.R. the support and sympathy of every colonial country. He envisioned an immense bloc stretching from the Pacific to Gibraltar and from New Guinea to the islands of the Red Sea.

Nikita felt that he could use the Suez situation to make up for his failure in the Belgrade affair.

"Listen," said Nikita to a diplomat at a banquet.[1] "Why do you wish to dominate the Arab nations? These nations belong to another culture. Western culture—mathematics and astronomy—came from the Arabs during the Crusades. The Arabs were slow to assimilate firearms, and the Arab world today owes its servitude to that slowness. But we will supply them with arms. We will arm them to combat injustice and liberate themselves. If war should break out over the Suez Canal, I would say to my son: 'Go there and fight as a volunteer. It is a war worth fighting. If you die on the battlefield, I'll be proud of you.'"

Astonished on hearing these remarks, the Western diplomat remarked: "Are you not afraid serious international complications might arise if Soviet volunteers were sent into Egypt? It is even said that a world war might ensue."

Nikita looked squarely at the diplomat. His eyes narrowed. He emptied his glass as if he needed more time to think about his answer.

"We have a nice proverb which Lenin was fond of repeating," said Nikita. "He even quoted it at the historic meeting of the Politbureau that voted to unleash the October Revolution. Here it is: 'One who is afraid of the wolves doesn't go into the woods.'"

The wily Ukrainian made many such speeches. He used pseudo-revolutionary language for the benefit of the Russian youth; the young people were tiring of the standard party-line jargon. Nikita wanted also to show the youth that aims worth fighting and dying for still existed. In 1875 thousands of young Russian students left Serbia and Montenegro to fight against the Turks. Nikita wished to rally the youth of the U.S.S.R. to his side.

On August 28, Khrushchev received Sokarno, the President of the Indonesian Republic, in Moscow and undertook to

[1] Reported by the Greek press.

negotiate economic and technical agreements (which were finally signed on September 16).

During his tour of Eastern Asia, Khrushchev made many speeches. The one made at Jakharta is typical:

"We are prepared to give the shirt off our back to our brothers in colonial countries. Come to us without fear. You will be helped, and there will be no obligation on your part. You are not asked to become communists. Go and offer your prayers to Allah and Mahomet if you wish, but let our engineers, our specialists, our doctors, our machines and our capital come to you. Yes, we have stores of gold. We promised you a loan of $500,000,000.00. We shall keep our promise.

"There is a Moslem in the Presidium of our communist party. Comrade Mukhittidinov is the youngest member of the Presidium. He is a communist, yet he goes to the Mosque every Friday. We should be happy to send him on a confidential mission to Jakharta someday."

Nikita also offered Russia's help in the fight against Dar-Ul-Islam's fanatical movement.

"Russia," said he, "would be able to send a first-class mediator to draw up a compromise. Mukhittidinov is a born diplomat. His ancestors were the Khan of Khiva's advisers."[1]

[1] Reported by the Greek press.

XXV

VICTORY IN KAZAKHSTAN

In the midst of international crises, Nikita found time to go to Kazakhstan to appraise at first hand the success of his great enterprise, the clearing of virgin lands.

He reasoned that it would be relatively easy for him to ward off the attacks of such enemies as Molotov, Malenkov and Kaganovitch as soon as the Kazakhstan enterprise proved to be a success. Old Kaganovitch seemed to forget that he had once sheltered the young colt Nikita, for he allied himself with Molotov, who was "the master's shadow."

Nikita knew that questions of international politics were of interest to only a small circle of the inhabitants of the U.S. S.R. and party members. Everyone else cared only about the "joyous and happy life" that they had been promised throughout so many years of hardships.

Kazakhstan wheat would have meant the belated attainment of one goal.

Putting these lands into cultivation was no easy task. There was nothing to work with: no dwellings, farm machinery, tractors, reapers, binders or thrashers. The new kolkhozes were thrown up on the open steppe, in the midst of packs of rats, martens and rabbits that roamed the Volga region. Men lived in tents like the Mormons who migrated to Salt Lake City. Some 500,000 young members of the Komsomols were mobilized by the Party, but they stole away from the kolkhozes in the dead of night and wandered through the steppe that reaches to the Caspian Sea and the Aral Sea and encompasses the Amu-Darya and Syr-Darya Rivers.

When asked why they were leaving, the young people replied: "Sure, it's nice to work all day long. But you have to have some fun, too. Here we don't even have one girl for twenty boys."

Nikita was apprised of their plight. "That's all right," he said. "In Ukrainia the girls have no boy-friends. They're ready to go to any lengths to find them. And the young Moslem boys of Central Asia do not become engaged because the sacred practice of *kalym*[1] lives on. The solution is obvious."

Suddenly matrimonial announcements filled Ukrainian newspapers. It was said that each girl who went to work in Kazakhstan would have the right to choose a husband from among ten young men who would be presented to her.[2]

And the young Moslems of Central Asia read announcements promising to find beautiful young brides for them (the newspapers printed photographs of beautiful Ukrainian girls) in the Kazakhstan kolkhozes.

A veritable matrimonial migration jammed the railway system between Ukrainia and the Caspian Sea. Carloads of prospective brides went to the Kazakhstan kolkhozes; prospective Moslem husbands swarmed in by the thousands.

The wily Ukrainian had promised marriage *after the harvest*. Like Swedish trial-marriages, this plan allowed couples

[1] The suitor pays a fixed sum to the parents of his future wife.
[2] Reported by the Moscow newspaper *Ogonio*.

sufficient time in which to become well acquainted. A special dowry was promised those who filled high quotas in their work.

When Nikita went to Central Asia to see the result of his stratagem, he had every reason to exult. Stalks of wheat covered the steppe where only weeds and hungry rodents had once been found. Now songs filled the air. Couples walked toward a big building hastily thrown up on the kolkhoz: the marriage-license bureau.

Nikita insisted on giving his personal benediction to some of the largest kolkhozes:

"I bless you, comrades and children. Live well and in perfect harmony! Those of you who desire the services of the Christian or Moslem clergy will be able to do so tomorrow."

The next day a priest and a mullah did arrive and bless those who asked for a blessing.

A spectacular festival was organized in the Lenin Kolkhoz. Two military orchestras had come from Tashkent on orders from Nikita. Swings, toboggans and a Ferris wheel were hastily erected.

Nikita wanted to make a speech befitting the occasion. Among other things, he said:[1]

"This will always be a historic land! *This is where we have carried off the greatest victory that the U.S.S.R. has ever known! 36,000,000 tons of surplus wheat will fill the storage bins of our nation!* This treasure is worth more than gold. No one will ever again know hunger in the U.S.S.R. No one! I made that promise and I am keeping my word. You, my friends, are the conquerors in the gigantic wheat battle."

The director of the kolkhoz came forward and shouted: "Hail to the commander-in-chief in the wheat battle, Comrade Nikita Sergyeyevitch Khrushchev!"

"Hurrah!" shouted the crowd.

[1] Reported by the Moscow newspaper *Ogonio*.

Nikita left for Moscow. The Suez crisis had reached its peak. The disorders in Poland foreshadowed grave developments. On September 9 Nasser rejected the Dulles plan for controlling the Suez Canal. He stated that he would never recognize the Association of Users of the Suez Canal.

Alarming rumors came from all sources. There was open talk of a military expedition to be organized by France and Great Britain to occupy the Canal zone, and a part of Egypt, too, perhaps. Soviet pilots arrived in Cairo on September 15, the very day on which Nasser chose to state that he would never agree to recognize the Association of Users of the Suez Canal. Clouds covered the sky. The rattling of arms in the small countries of the Near East presaged, as always, military conflagrations among the great powers.

Shukri-Al-Kuatli, the president of the Syrian Republic, announced his coming trip to Moscow. Colonel Abdel-Hamid-Serraj, assumed de facto control of Syria and prepared to arrest his opponents and turn them over to the Court Martial.

The embassies and press agencies were in turmoil. Everyone wanted to know the real intentions of the boss, Nikita Khrushchev.

He was not shy. He talked a steady stream, especially at banquets after several glasses of champagne or vodka.

"I like French champagne very much," he said. "The French have nice things. But what do they have against Egypt?"

"They ask only for free passage through the Suez Canal," replied a South American diplomat.

Nikita looked surprised.

"What? They want free passage through the Suez Canal? They have free passage right. Nasser doesn't bother their ships. They don't even pay tolls. They are gate-crashers."

"France asks for a firm guarantee of free passage. She will

never agree to be at the mercy of a man like Nasser. His word is not enough."

Nikita then drew near a Russian-speaking Finnish diplomat and said:

"Who knows? Perhaps the French are right. Have you heard the latest news broadcast by the British station in Cyprus in Arabic and beamed to Egypt? Keep it to yourself. I have already been accused of being a hardened anti-Semite. And still, when I was young, I defended the Jews during the pogroms in the Ukraine. Later I prevented Stalin from deporting all Jews in the U.S.S.R. to the Soviet Far East, to Birobijan. But now the English are saying: 'People of Egypt, rise up against this infamous Nasser, for he is a converted Jew whose real name is Khaim Gamalovh!'"

Nikita laughed heartily and poured himself another glass. He continued:

"The Britons are sly ones. They accept Jews as prime ministers at home. Without Disraeli, the Suez Canal would never have fallen into English hands. The story of Disraeli and Rothschild is well known. But the Britons would like to keep the Egyptians from having a president of Jewish origin."

When the stupefied diplomat asked the source of such a statement, Nikita, jovial and laughing, told him to ask Sir Anthony who was in charge at Cyprus.

Thereupon Nikita withdrew[1] and left for the meeting of the Presidium of the Central Committee at which Ponomarenko and Koniev were to report on the Polish situation.

He knew that he would be attacked harshly. But his reply was well prepared. He had carried away an unheard of triumph in Kazakhstan. He had won a victory in the wheat battle, and one that Stalin had never been able to win despite his despotism. Hundreds of thousands of human corpses had

[1] Reported by the Argentine press.

rotted on the steppes of Western Siberia where Stalin had tried in vain for ten years to clear some 1,000,000 hectars of virgin land. Against this, Khrushchev had cleared 25,000,000 hectars in two years—and had left no victims or skeletons on the steppe.

Nikita had already prepared his answer to the Presidium of the Supreme Soviet and to the whole world:

"When the wheat-bins are full, it is easy to get whatever you want from your friends or enemies. I am the one who filled the bins!"[1]

[1] Reported by the French press.

XXVI

NEW TALKS WITH TITO

Khrushchev sorely needed his Kazakhstan triumph in his struggle against his enemies on the Presidium. Pospelov, the third secretary, had formed a small Stalinist circle within the central committee of the secretariat; these men took great pains to obtain from Molotov and others documentation concerning the "fatal mistakes" of Nikita. After the nineteenth congress of the Party, Stalin had slated Pospelov for a position of leadership. Pospelov was a hard-core Stalinist and a close friend of General Poskrebychev. He was a harsh man, scholarly by nature, and a staunch theorist. It was hard for him to accept the co-operative leadership championed by Nikita. He took it upon himself to show that Nikita's flirtation with Tito was but the beginning of an "ideological fall leading straight into the bourgeois slough." Supported by Michael Susslov, second secretary of the central committee, Pospelov presented to the Presidium a report on "the catastrophic collapse of Marxist-Leninist ideology among the parties of the people's democracies."

He concluded by denouncing Yugoslavia as the center of the new bourgeois heresy.

The newspaper of the Central Committee, the *Kommunist,* which was edited by Pospelov, published a vague but symptomatic article. The article pointed up the "perfidious attempts tending to hold up the worst samples of Yugoslav nationalist deviation as an example of a return to Marxism-Leninism."

The French communist party supported these attacks. Ever since the Congress of Le Havre, when Michael Susslov attended as the Kremlin's representative, Thorez' party had taken a firm stand on the side of the hard-core Communists and against Nikita. Its opposition to the Kremlin's neo-liberalism put Khrushchev in a difficult situation.

Nikita decided to pay Tito another visit in an attempt to effect a compromise.

On September 19, 1956, Nikita Khrushchev surprised the world by landing at Belgrade in his four-engined T-14.

The announcement was so sensational that it eclipsed the news of the opening of the second conference on the Suez Canal at Lancaster House on the same day. The eighteen-nation conference had been called for the purpose of approving the charter of the Association of Users of the Suez Canal.

"Why had Nikita gone to see Tito?"

That was the question asked by the world press. That was the only topic of conversation. Everybody was talking about Nikita, the Kremlin's upstart child.

Nikita and Tito did everything possible to camouflage the real purpose of his trip.

"I have simply come for a rest at my friend's home," Nikita declared, "and to hunt in the mountains."

And indeed, the two statesmen did soon start on a hunting trip that was singularly reminiscent of the pre-World War II diplomatic hunts.

Nikita's hunting vacation lasted only about a week. On September 27, a telegram from Belgrade announced that Marshal Tito and Madame Jovanka Broz would accompany Nikita to the Crimea:

"I am going to rest and hunt in the Crimea," declared Tito.

The excitement continued. Pictures published in the world press showed Nikita beside Tito, facing a huge mountain stag felled by the Marshal. Both hunters were shown admiring the splendid catch.

But more was at stake than stags. As if by sheer coincidence, the Crimean coast filled with members of the Central Committee of the Russian communist party. They all came to spend their vacation there. A secret conference was held in the luxurious palace of Prince Yussupov, Grigoryi Rasputin's assassin. Pospelov and Susslov drew up the minutes of the conversations.

Molotov, who had arrived in Yalta from Sukhumi, stated the problem with brutal frankness. He was supported by Malenkov, Kaganovitch, Shvernik, Susslov, Saburov and Pervukhin. Old Voroshilov, while he supported Nikita, shifted from one camp to the other.

"What the socialist camp won in the war against Hitler must not be given up to the capitalist camp."[1]

Voroshilov's terse statement meant that the U.S.S.R. categorically refused to free the satellite countries and that *any attempt to bring about emancipation by force might actually constitute a* causus belli.

"I also advocate socialism," replied Tito. "But each socialist country must have the right to define the road that leads to socialism. Comrade Khrushchev has expressed his agreement with me on this point."

But Molotov was not easily convinced.

"I do not share Comrade Khrushchev's opinion. The peo-

[1] The *Red Star*, September 29, 1956.

ple's democracies can not be left as sole judges of their political course. The U.S.S.R. has a 'blood' right over them. We lost 17,000,000 human lives in the war against the Third Reich."

"These high losses were due to Stalin," Tito answered dryly. "He failed to foresee the war. Yugoslavia also lost many human lives. Poland suffered from the Nazis relatively more than the U.S.S.R."[1]

Molotov concluded: "We can never allow the leading role of the U.S.S.R. in the world communist movement to be disputed. This is a matter of life and death insofar as Lenin's work is concerned. *We wish to preserve the right to correct errors and harmful deviations.*"

In the ensuing duel, Tito retorted: "Lenin was actually speaking of nationalist deviations. He said that the chauvinism of comrades in great countries is more dangerous than the nationalism of small oppressed countries."

"You cited that statement once before and you distorted it!" shouted Molotov. "It has no place in our discussion. The U.S. S.R. does not use imperialistic oppression against small nations."

Tito shrugged his shoulders. Certainly he must have remembered that a Yugoslav delegation, which had gone to Moscow to sign an economic treaty, could testify to his arrogance and his dictatorial tone. When he submitted the text of the treaty for their signatures, without even giving them a chance to discuss it freely, he seemed to be handing a *diktat* to a conquered nation and not an agreement with a friendly country.[2]

The Marshal from Belgrade stood up.

"You have to win the confidence of the people's democracies, Comrade Molotov," he said. "You have to achieve

[1] Reported by Deajer.
[2] *Ibid.*

friendly and benevolent co-operation, not blind obedience. As for me, I could not sign an agreement acknowledging that the U.S.S.R. has the right to impose its viewpoint on the people's democracies. That would contradict the principle of complete equality among large and small countries, which is the essence of Leninism. I am a Leninist and shall remain one until the end."

A cold gust forced the window of the Yussupov Palace half-open. The wind came from the Chatyr-Dag Mountains where Czar Alexander III liked to hunt.

And the wind seemed to bring with it something from the old imperialistic and Czarist Russia and inject it into the discussion between two men, each of whom believed that he was "a true Leninist."

Tito went back to Belgrade *without having signed the socialist submission* asked of him by Molotov.

XXVII

NEW TROUBLES IN POLAND

October came. A conference between eighteen ambassadors had been initiated in London on October 1. At last the Association of Users of the Suez Canal was organized. A few days later, on October 6, funeral services were held for Laszlo Rajk in Budapest. The Poznan trials completely discredited Polish Stalinism.

Ambassador Ponomarenko again arrived in the Soviet capital. He was the bearer of very bad news. On October 19, the plenary session of the Central Committee of the Unified Polish Workers Party was to meet in Warsaw. Ponomarenko had been told that the majority of the Polish Central Committee had decided on a decisive about-face: Gomulka was to be elected to the Politbureau and was to become First Secretary of the Central Committee. The Stalinists of the Natoline group were to be eliminated. The new leadership of the Party and the Polish Nation would announce *Poland's withdrawal from the Warsaw Pact and would ask for the evacuation of Russian troops.*

During a dramatic session of the Presidium, Ponomarenko presented his report.

Khrushchev took the lead.

"I shall personally strangle the first Polish communist who proves to be a traitor!" he shouted. "But can we be sure of this plot? I can hardly believe such treachery possible."

Ponomarenko pretended that he had in his pocket a sworn statement made by a high-ranking Polish official who was in a position to know Polish politics and who had overheard a conversation between Gomulka, Ochab and Cyrankievitch.

Spurred by the gravity of the situation, the members of the Presidium decided to act. They had the support of the army. Rokossovsky was asked to use his troops and the security troop to occupy Warsaw if necessary.

Ponomarenko was ordered to return to Warsaw immediately. A special delegation left shortly thereafter to attend the meeting of the Polish central committee. The delegation had the authority to make an on-the-spot decision concerning the possibility of military intervention.

On October 19, Khruschev arrived at Mokotovo Airport near Warsaw. Accompanying him were Molotov, Mikoyan and Susslov.

A delegation of the Central Committee of the Unified Polish Workers Party was present at the airport to greet the Soviet leaders.

Nikita left the plane first. He wanted to impress everyone with his intransigence in matters affecting the Soviet state. He knew that Marshal Zhukov was supposed to arrive incognito that very day for a personal inspection of the Soviet military set-up and a conference with Rokossovsky and Koniev. It was possible that units of the Polish Army would refuse to follow Rokossovsky. Plans had to be made to cover any eventuality.

"You are traitors!" Nikita shot at the Polish communists

from the airport. He refused to shake Gomulka's hand. "You are trying to take Poland out of the socialist bloc. You are trying to surrender your country to the Americans and the Zionists. You forget that the U.S.S.R. lost millions of lives in liberating you from Hitler's yoke and in winning back your territory in Pomerania, Silesia and Brandenburg!"[1]

Gomulka stammered a few words. His face was ashen.

The discussion between the Soviet delegation and the Polish leaders was conducted in the Belvedere Palace. A huge room that had once served Grand Duke Constantine, the Governor General of Poland in 1830, as a banquet room had been refurbished for permanent use as a conference hall. Ponomarenko was present. His aides came and went, bringing a steady stream of reports on the temperament of the Polish capital.

Mikoyan had a reputation of softness. To him Nikita gave the leading role in the debates.

"You are stupid renegades!" shouted Mikoyan. "You forget the ABC's of communism."

Vladislas Gomulka calmly replied: "Stalin had the ABC's of communism shot."[2]

An adviser from the soviet embassy in Warsaw arrived with bad news: workers in the Zeran Automobile Plant had banded together and taken up arms. Students were also taking up arms. Security troops led by General Komar, recently released from prison, refused to march against the bands of workers. The regular Polish troops were unanimously against Rokossovsky.

In a small room near the conference hall, Marshal Koniev discussed plans for a new Battle of Warsaw with Rokossovsky. He wanted to call in Soviet troops garrisoned in military districts of Byelorussia and Ukrainia. Zhukov opposed Ko-

[1] Reported by members of the press who were present at the airport.
[2] A pun: Bukharin was the author of the book, *The A.B.C.'s of Communism;* Stalin had him executed.

niev's plan. Reliable Soviet and Polish witnesses report that he said:

"That would precipitate a battle at the border, for the Poles would oppose the entry of these troops. We must wait for the result of the political conference."

Thereupon Koniev proposed that troops stationed in Eastern Germany be ordered to march into Poland.

Zhukov opposed this plan, too. He feared an uprising in East Germany. An uprising there could have marked the beginning of a generalized conflict.

The conference went on inside the palace. Outside, in Lazienki Park, barren trees shivered and dead leaves rustled. Nikita's voice grew hoarse. He talked on and on, trying to convince Ochab and Cyrankievitch of the necessity of admitting several members of the Natoline group to the Politbureau, and especially of not excluding Marshal Rokossovsky from the Politbureau.

"That is my last word," said Nikita. "If you refuse, a break will be imminent."

He struck the table with his fist. He wanted this to be the gesture used by a diplomat to clinch an argument at a conference of world-wide importance. But there was something in his gesture reminiscent of the huckstering scenes at the Sorotchinsky fair in the Ukraine, brilliantly described by Gogol.

The Poles asked for a break in the conference to allow them to consult the plenary session of their party's central committee.

"No!" shouted Mikoyan. "You must answer immediately. Yes or no. A compromise is a breach!"[1]

A heavy silence fell on the hall. Gomulka's face expressed his irrevocable will.

[1] Reported by the Polish and French press (Mr. Ben).

Suddenly Ponomarenko appeared. He went over to Khrushchev and handed him a note.

"A telegram from Mao-Tse-Tung. He asks us to avoid the use of any force at Warsaw."

The die was cast. Nikita started back to Moscow, leaving the Polish Workers Party's Central Committee free to elect a new Politbureau. Stalinists were excluded from it. On October 28 Marshal Rokossovsky was relieved of his duties as Minister of Defense and Commander-in-Chief of the Polish Army.

But five days before his discharge, on October 23, 1956 Khrushchev had to face another test: the Budapest uprising occurred.

XXVIII

THE HUNGARIAN UPRISING

Neither Nikita nor his colleagues could grasp the significance of the event in time. They firmly believed that the troubles that had broken out in the Hungarian capital could be solved by the election of a new secretary and the nomination of a new president of the Council.

Imre Nagy became President of the Council, replacing Hegedus, and Janos Kadar replaced Geroe as First Secretary of the Communist Party on October 25.

But something else had happened during the short interval: on October 23, before reliquishing his duties, Ernst Geroe had appealed directly to Marshal Koniev and to General Gribennik, who commanded the Russian units stationed in Hungaria. He asked the Russians to intervene. Marshal Koniev was glad to accede to his request.

The Russians intervened after Nagy became President of the Council. The Hungarian people held Nagy responsible for the Russian intervention which robbed him of all authority.

The Hungarian uprising did not stop with the formation of Nagy's government. The nation came closer and closer to a state of anarchy.

A large-scale diplomatic reception took place in Moscow during the historic days marking the end of October and the beginning of November. Conversation was focused on the Israeli invasion of Egypt and the Hungarian uprising.

All the leading figures of the Kremlin were there, including Nikita. Foreign diplomats tried to determine how the Kremlin really looked on the situation.

Dimitri Shepilov was curt and laconic. The Russian Minister of Foreign Affairs had retained all his short-comings as a journalist and had not yet acquired the qualities of a leader in the field of external politics. Answering questions about the Hungarian situation, he said:

"Some small-scale looting and banditry, nothing more. You talk about a revolution in Hungary? My answer is this: the world still goes 'round!"[1]

Shepilov was trying to ridicule those who took the Hungarian events seriously. But he must have remembered that the world was also turning even during the October Revolution of 1917.

Hearing what his Minister of Foreign Affairs had said, Nikita added:

"The Hungarians have always doted on trouble. The Rakosi-Geroe clique oppressed the country too much through its stupid police dictatorship. Imre Nagy will change things. He is a good man. We know him very well. Personally, I held him in high esteem when he was a professor of rural sociology at the Academy of Agriculture in Moscow in 1940."

[1] Spoken at the Belgian Embassy.

Leaving the circle grouped around Shepilov, Nikita approached the ambassador of a Western power.

The ambassador, who spoke Russian fairly well, asked him:

"And if the Hungarians asked for outright independence, what would your attitude be?"

Nikita winked slyly:

"You will not repeat my answer to His Excellency Dimitri Shepilov?"

"You have my word, Mr. Khrushchev."

"Then I'll tell you that I made up my mind a long time ago. If Hungary became a second Finland, there would be no objection on my part. I speak for myself, not for my colleagues, Mr. Ambassador. Finland gives us every guarantee we asked for. She will never take part in any act directed against the U.S.S.R. And still, she is not a member of the Eastern bloc. But Hungary's emancipation does not have to take place in one month, or even in a year. You know the saying: 'All things come to him who waits.' " He ended by saying: "We have a nice Russian proverb, too: 'The one who rushes is the laughing-stock of the world.' "

The ambassador could have told Nikita that the tragic happenings in Hungary could never make the world laugh. But he was satisfied simply to note the opinion of the Number One man of the Kremlin, for it suggested that the Hungarian drama would eventually be resolved peaceably.

On October 31 something unexpected happened: Cardinal Mindszenty, freed by the Hungarian Army on October 30, made a public speech.

The Cardinal stated that Nagy's communist government could not satisfy the country. He stressed that the Russian military occupation must cease immediately. He proclaimed the necessity of guaranteeing the union of Hungary and Austria.

On the evening of October 31, Koniev's order, counter-signed by Zhukov, started troops moving into Hungary from East Germany and from the Russian-Hungarian border.

The Presidium of the Central Committee of the Russian Communist Party was forced to approve the decision of the military authorities of the U.S.S.R. The Soviet security system of Central Europe was threatened with collapse. If one dent were made in the system, every country in the Eastern bloc might rise up against Russian domination, break away from the U.S.S.R., and ally themselves with the hostile bloc. The State Department repeatedly emphasized that the U.S.A. had no intention of bringing the countries that wished to break away from the Warsaw Pact into its zone of influence. But Radio Munich took a different course.

It broadcast a direct call to revolt to every Russian satellite. In the Rumanian, Bulgarian and German universities, students banded together in support of the freedom movement of the Hungarian students who were fighting off Soviet attacks from their barricades in Budapest.

Khrushchev and the Presidium of the Central Committee grasped the importance of the situation: if they gave in to the Budapest insurgents, an anti-government movement might well be directed against the U.S.S.R. itself. For as a multinational country, the U.S.S.R. might run the risk of being splintered. The Army, representing the new ruling caste, had come through the war against the Third Reich victoriously; it could not allow "Lenin's heritage" and the "empire created by the Georgian" to crumble away; it would act, militarily and politically, if necessary.

On November 2, 1956, Nikita called an extraordinary meeting. He wanted to consult every Soviet marshal in Moscow.

Nikita Khrushchev put the Hungarian problem in their hands.

There was no longer any doubt about what was happening

in Budapest. Nagy was losing whatever authority he had left. Several thousand insurgents, led by Jano Dudas, who was one of the leaders of the revolutionary committee, had shown its hostility toward the President of the Council. Two different groups had entered the Ministry of Foreign Affairs and pillaged the archives.

In an attempt to salvage his prestige, Nagy proclaimed Hungary's withdrawal from the Warsaw Pact on November 1; he declared that his country was neutral and asked the U.N.O. to guarantee its neutrality. The President of the Council also proceeded to reshuffle his government and bring in people known to have anti-Russian inclinations. He proclaimed Western-style elections, free and democratic, to give *all parties, without exception,* an opportunity to participate. In the atmosphere created by the anti-Russian revolt, such an election would inevitably produce a parliament so hostile to the U.S.S.R. as to rule out any possibility of the neutralization of Hungary. A conference between "B-K" and the marshals resulted in this decision: *the revolt must be crushed.* As in 1849, following Kossuth's revolt, Russian divisions marched into Hungary.

On November 4, 1956, Soviet troops occupied Budapest. Nagy sought asylum in the Yugoslav Legation. The First Secretary of the Hungarian Communist Party, Janos Kadar, formed a weak puppet-government.

The same day, on November 4, 1956, French and British forces had landed at Port Saïd and Port Fuad.

The Soviet government had thought that the decision to use massive intervention in Hungary would effect a quick solution. Janos Kadar was as anti-Stalin as Nagy. He had suffered more than Nagy, for he had been the victim of ignominious torture in the jails of Farkas. Three days after the Russian intervention Nikita attended a diplomatic reception. There he declared:

"Now I see clearly that the Hungarian revolt was the work of fascists and not of the people as a whole. If the revolt had been truly a popular one, our army could not have checked it in three days."

Nikita's statement was rather rash. The Hungarian revolt was by no means checked in three days, even with Soviet tanks surrounding the capital. The workers on Csepel Island continued the struggle. The workers at Pecs, Debrecen, Szegesfekervar and Gyoergy refused to put down their arms in spite of the promises and appeals of Kadar. Workers' committees became the organs of a provisional government.

XXIX

CONCLUSION

The popular nature of the Hungarian uprising was obvious. The U.S.S.R., censured by the U.N.O., suffered a great loss of prestige in the Afro-Asian countries which "B-K" had won over in their trip through Asia. A number of foreign communist parties broke away from the Kremlin. Within the Presidium of the Central Committee, Nikita was attacked by the hard-core Stalinists for his laxity in allowing his secret report to be divulged to Tito and the fast rate at which de-Stalinization was being pursued.

But the wily Ukrainian was a master of self-defense. He tried to show that the Polish and Hungarian episodes resulted mainly from discontent among the masses and that their low standard of living was due to Stalin's regime.

He claimed credit for finally, forty years after the revolution, having raised the standard of living to such a high level that the U.S.S.R. no longer had to fear a revolt.

Nikita Khrushchev pointed out that Kazakhstan wheat and Siberian corn would make it possible for the Russians to have more livestock and thus be assured of living better than in Stalin's time. As for dissatisfaction among the intellectuals and the danger of a Soviet "Pitoefi" circle, Nikita proposed to name Molotov "Grand Inquisitioner of Letters, Arts and Culture," and also nominated him as Minister of State Control to combat bureaucracy.

When he made the last proposal, which was a concession to the hard-core faction, Nikita would have had a good laugh if he had remembered Bukharin's words:

"Comrade Molotov is known as the Number 1 bureaucrat of the U.S.S.R."

When visiting student gatherings, Nikita had warned:

"If you are dissatisfied with the government, you can quit school and go to work. There are plenty of openings in the Asiatic kolkhozes and in the Siberian mines. Your stipends are larger than the salaries of unskilled workers, and it would be easy to find replacements for you."[1]

The threat of expulsion was enough to keep down anti-governmental movements in the universities.

Finally, taking the bull by the horns, Nikita expounded his views on anti-Stalinism:

"I have never said that Stalin was a bad Marxist-Leninist. I have spoken of his errors as a person and of the cult of personality which he astutely favored. But Stalin knew how to defeat our enemies. And in that sense I am also a Stalinist. I shall never hesitate to use violence to save Lenin's work!"[2]

Such was the frank explanation given by Nikita to his critics on the presidium. His explanation resembled the self-criticism which is the keystone of the Soviet system. Yet his was not true self-criticism. He had no intention of renouncing the de-Stalinization policy outlined by the twentieth congress of the Russian communist party.

He simply needed the official blessing of foreign communist parties; he wanted recognition of Russia's right to leader-

[1] Reported by *Pravda*.
[2] Also reported by *Pravda*.

ship of the communist world. Molotov and his supporters had accused Nikita of having wasted the moral heritage of the Russian communist party on the International Workers Movement.

Finally, to show all satellite countries that they could no longer expect the support of Red China in case of a rebellion on their part, and to warn Gomulka against emancipating Poland (which he had already rescued from Soviet bayonets once) too brusquely and too completely, Nikita called in Chou-En-Lai. The head of the Chinese government visited Moscow, Warsaw and other capitals of the satellite countries.

Chou-En-Lai, the representative of a vast country boasting a population of 600,000,000, a rapidly growing industry, and an army tested on the battlefields of Korea, bowed to Khrushchev, the heir to Lenin and Stalin.

This symbolic pledge of allegiance on the part of Red China was given in exchange for new economic and financial concessions promised by Nikita. Chou-En-Lai's visit was a historic event for still another reason: thanks to Nikita, Red China became a mediator in Central Europe as well as in the Far East.

The Ukrainian had taken every precautionary measure. He could now brave the fatidic plenary session of the Central Committee of the Russian Communist Party. The session had been adjourned since October, for Nikita knew that Molotov and his friends were ready to present a resolution to discharge him from his post.

A foreign diplomat asked him whether the rumors concerning his coming resignation were actually true. Nikita answered:

"I neither confirm nor deny the rumors. You complain of censorship and say that you are prevented from reporting sensational news to your readers. You may print anything you choose about me. Fire me if you like. The censors have orders to take no part in the duel between me and the world press."

"Then you know what the world press is saying about you, Mr. Khrushchev?"

Nikita smiled:

"I read non-Soviet dispatches. I am forced to. But I swear that it brings me no great pleasure to do so."[1]

❋   ❋   ❋   ❋   ❋

The plenary meeting of the Central Committee was held in January, 1957. It ended without Nikita's having been discharged. The international press had indulged in wild speculations, but the only major change was the replacement of Saburov, the champion of state planning, by Pervukhin, who was Nikita's favorite.

Encroaching on the territory of his minister of foreign affairs, Nikita set to work. He wished to bring the U.S.S.R. out of the state of diplomatic isolation that had resulted from the Hungarian situation.

The international situation was no longer as favorable to the soft approach as it had been in the blissful days of the Geneva conference. The Eisenhower Doctrine caused a bitter controversy between Washington and Moscow.

"I'm afraid we are pulling chestnuts from the Anglo-French fire in the Near East and handing them over to the United States," said Nikita one day.

Khrushchev then turned his attention to Central Europe and to the German problem, always vital to the security of the U.S.S.R.

His ambassador to Bonn, Mr. Smirnov, had stayed in Moscow for a long time without having received any new instructions. The German elections were drawing near. In a private conversation, Nikita had put forth an idea:

[1] Reported by the Swiss press.

"Why not repeat Bismarck's experiment in our attempt to bring about the unification of Germany? We could begin by setting up a confederation of the two Germanies, East Germany and West Germany. They could constitute a common market but have different social systems; this arrangement could work indefinitely; it would offer a practical solution to the question of German unity. A security pact between NATO and the countries that signed the Warsaw agreement, together with an agreement on disarmament, could stabilize the Central European situation once and for all. . . ."

Walter Ulbricht was authorized to make a public statement concerning a plan for an East-West German Confederation.[1] Nikita Khrushchev still clung to his brain-child, the easing of international tensions, in spite of the events of 1956.

His plan was to bring about massive disarmament. He believed that this would allow Russia to become a prosperous country in fifteen years and thus attract the Afro-Asian countries.

But Nikita failed to consider the psychological and social changes that would result from prosperity. A flourishing economy needs no one to dominate its culture; nor is there any reason for it to continue to feed millions of hungry bureaucrats.

Nikita did not worry much over these questions, just as he had not paid much attention to the consequences of his secret report. He is an inveterate pragmatist. As the off-spring of an impoverished peasantry, he has but one aim: prosperity. He feels that all other problems will take care of themselves.

After his visit to Kazakhstan in 1956, he had said:

"I am from the Kursk region. It is known throughout Russia for its nightingales. We are proud of our Kursk nightingales.

"I hope that you will be happy here and that you will

---

[1] He spoke of it on two different occasions in 1957.

create a life of ease and enjoyment. When everything is finished, let me know. I shall send you several thousand Kursk nightingales to sing in your gardens."

He stopped, filled a glass with water, and added:

"At the moment, I can only ask you to listen to me, not to the Kursk nightingales."

*   *   *   *   *

Nikita had begun his political career in the atmosphere of Russian "neo-messianism," which Lenin had stimulated by his dogma of world-wide revolution. He had lived during the Stalin era, when Russian "neo-Messianism" had become oddly mingled with the most blatant chauvinism. For example, Potapov, one of the young communists, wrote a letter to Stalin, in which he said:

"We are a people of genius. The Russian people has produced the greatest scholars, the greatest authors, the greatest inventors, the greatest sociologists and economists, the greatest generals and the greatest statesmen," and he concluded his letter by declaring:

"And to crown all, we have given Stalin to the world."

When quoting this letter now, Nikita generally omits this last sentence. But, otherwise, his ideas are still very close to those of Potapov. He is still influenced by "neo-messianism" and the blatant chauvinism of the Stalin era. A self-made man and a sincere Marxist, he is fully convinced that he has a monopoly of the truth.

"You refuse to admit that I am right," he said to Dr. Adenauer. "You intend to persist in your alliance with the capitalist countries. This will soon bring you to your grave."

The impetuous "ataman" probably did not realize that this was hardly a tactful way to speak to an old man of eighty-two.

But he no doubt remembered the "political science"[1] which he had studied at the time of Lenin, and also the remark made by Lenin in 1919: "Capitalism is moving rapidly towards its grave." If Dr. Adenauer had attended the school of political science, he would have known the origin of Nikita's assertion, and he might have reminded the "ataman" of the Soviet Union that forty years had elapsed since that remark was made, and that capitalism, far from landing in its grave, had undergone a process of evolution and change. He might also have added that Lenin's régime had undergone a similar process, and that the state capitalism, with its bureaucracy, which prevailed under Khrushchev differed more from Lenin's régime than Roosevelt's planned economy from the economic anarchy of Herbert Hoover. Dr. Adenauer made no such remark. But Nikita himself did. In the course of a "frank discussion" with a group of Americans, and startled by the account of economic and social life in the United States which they had given, he exclaimed:

If all that is true, it may well be that we are advancing towards the same goal, but will reach it by different routes.

Shepilov, Nikita's alter ego, hastened to straighten out and gloze over what Nikita had said, by interpreting it in "dialectical" terms in the columns of *The Communist,* thus:

The political meaning of the same social measures adopted in the Soviet Union and in the capitalist countries respectively is different. While in the Soviet Union the introduction of a thirty-hour week would have meant an enormous advance towards communism, the same measure in the United States would merely be an attempt by the capitalists to corrupt the working-class so as to stave off the advent of the socialist régime.

[1] This "political science" was studied at the time of Lenin by every member of the bolshevik party at a special school, known as the school of political science. Students of this rather sketchy science had to learn by heart numerous quotations from Karl Marx, Friedrich Engels, Lenin and Trotsky.

What does Nikita think when he reads this sample of pseudo-Marxist "dialectic"? This must remain a matter for guess-work, for Nikita was born in a country where Kuzma Prutkov, the "leg-pulling philosopher," summed up the pivotal idea of his system of philosophy for all self-taught Russian revolutionaries in the following illustrative example:

If you saw an elephant in a cage labelled "bull," you should not believe the evidence of your own eyes. The label is more important than the thing that is labelled.

Nikita sticks to this system of philosophy and continues to take at its face value Shepilov's label on the cage of the capitalistic world, in spite of the fact that this world puts into practice on a large scale the principles of a planned and guided economy, as well as such measures as the minimum wage, health and unemployment insurance and so forth. All the same, there must be times when, in his heart of hearts, the first secretary of the Russian communist party cannot help asking himself whether the "dialectical philosophy" of such thinkers as Shepilov and Kuzma Prutkov is to be taken seriously. The younger and succeeding soviet generations will ask themselves the same question. The appalling example of the Stalin period, the seamy side of which has so recently been disclosed by Nikita himself, will help to provide them with fresh food for thought.

The younger soviet generations, who have been to school, are beginning to understand what things are really like on the other side of the iron curtain, and, after having repudiated the truth of Stalinism, they might well have their doubts about the truth of "dialectical philosophy." Should this happen, the name of Nikita Khrushchev, the iconoclast of Stalinism, will be identified with a new era in the history of Soviet Russia. Will the Khrushchev era bring relief to the Russian people?

XXX

EPILOGUE

How Nikita Khrushchev the Ukrainian Ataman Delivered the Coup de Grace to the Old-Guard Stalinists

The plenary session of the central committee of the Russian communist party which ended in Moscow on June 29 with the condemnation of "the anti-party heresy of Malenkov, Molotov, Kaganovitch" and their fellow-traveler Shepilov, may well be an important landmark in the history of the U.S.S.R.

This action marked a decisive victory for Khrushchev in his struggle for control of the party machinery. The political structure of the Soviet Union was still the same as it had been during the Georgian's regime: it was under the dictatorship of a single party, the communist party. Whoever dominated this party became, *ipso facto,* the ruler of the nation. To be sure, the twentieth congress had given its stamp of approval to collective leadership through the Presidium of the central committee of the Party, the "secret directorate" of the nation. The cult of personality was "definitely condemned" and

Stalinist errors were made public. But it is obvious that, so long as control of the U.S.S.R. depends on the dictatorship of a single party, collective leadership can function normally only if there is a "supreme arbiter" on the Presidium. Nikita Khrushchev wanted to be the supreme arbiter. He had all the necessary qualifications, having been educated in the great Stalin's entourage. "I am proud of having grown up under Stalin," he once confided after a banquet in the Kremlin.

But the ebullient Nikita is too impulsive by nature to be a veritable supreme arbiter. He is too fond of taking the initiative in instances which appear at times to endanger the preservation of the existing regime in the U.S.S.R. His blustering reconciliation with Tito, some of his undertakings in external politics, his speeches delivered while under the influence of alcohol—all of this went against the grain of men like Molotov and Kaganovitch, who were brought up in the esoteric school of Stalin, in which sincerity in general was ruled out as a "survival of out-moded capitalism."

Nikita understood the danger confronting him. That is why he followed methodically the policy of nominating hand-picked men to the posts of secretaries of the local parties. It was for the same reason that he allied himself closely to Nicolas Bulganin in driving Malenkov out of the presidency of the council. At the twentieth congress Nikita had enough support to change the composition of the Presidium of the central committee by placing on it a majority of members faithful to himself. Though he had reached only the half-way point when he took Stalin's place on the central committee of the party, Nikita had inherited the dictator's patience. Before leaping into the final struggle, he was awaiting a victory in the wheat battle; he wanted to clear the virgin fields of Kazakhstan and create a solid base for the Soviet economy.

There, he was phenomenally successful. When developments in Poland and Hungary caused the formation of the

Molotov-Kaganovitch anti-party coalition in the fall of 1956, Nikita Khrushchev could boast of clearing 25,000,000 hectares of virgin fields and a goodly store of grain in the bins.

But this much should be remembered: that he managed to paralyze his adversaries in December, 1956, after the plenary session of the central committee, is explained by his alliance with three other members of the Presidium. These three were: Bulganin, the head of the government and of the bureaucrats comprising the different ministries; Mikoyan, one of the leaders of the "economists," whose famous speech against Stalin at the twentieth congress keynoted Khrushchev's secret report; and Marshal Zhukov, the head of the Soviet armed forces.

Khrushchev's enemies, Molotov and Kaganovitch (his former boss), had but one noteworthy associate, Malenkov, who was embittered over his forced resignation from the presidency of the council and the humiliating statement that he was obliged to sign before his departure. In his statement, he admitted his administrative short-comings, real and imaginary. He was a valuable ally for Molotov since he was backed by a segment of the party bureaucrats and the corps of "economists" who had come, like Malenkov, from the advanced school of technology: Saburov, the president of the Gosplan; Pervukhin, the minister of hydroelectric centers; Malychev and many others. All these old-line members of the Soviet hierarchy grouped themselves around one Georgi Maximilianovitch Malenkov. Another occasional ally rallied to the support of the Molotov-Kaganovitch partnership: Dimitri Shepilov, ex-minister of foreign affairs of the U S.S.R. and friend of Colonel Nasser.

* * * * *

It is possible that the anti-party opposition led by Molotov and Kaganovitch would never have been proclaimed openly if Mao-Tse-Tung had not one day undertaken his "get-tough" maneuver. The hard-core coalition had seen in this maneuver the possibility of reshaping the situation in the U.S.S.R. and removing the ebullient Nikita from his post.

This whole subtle play within the Kremlin sprang from the Molotov-Kaganovitch bid to eliminate Nikita and effect a wholesale replacement of the personnel of his secretariat. According to well-informed sources, *Molotov was to be named first secretary of the central committee, Kaganovitch second, and Shepilov third, while Malenkov was to be returned to his post as president of the council. Such was the "plot" mentioned by Pravda.*

Nikita took the initiative. In self-defense, he attacked his adversaries. He used as a pretext the private gatherings of member-delegates of the central committee of the party sponsored by Molotov-Kaganovitch; at these meetings, Khrushchev's "errors" were supposed to have been discussed. Private meetings of this type during the plenary session of the central committee were not outlawed by the Russian communist party as a rule, but the secretariat of the central committee (Khrushchev, that is) had labeled them "shameful anti-party intrigues against collective leadership." The plenary meeting of the central committee scheduled to end around June 25 was prolonged for several days, resulting in the adjournment of the Prague visit set for July 2 by Khrushchev and Bulganin.

The drama unfolded in accordance with the pattern set by Malenkov's dismissal. The plenary session of the central committee adopted a motion designating the guilty ones as "anti-party" and "anti-Leninist" and expelling them from the Presidium of the central committee. The Presidium was changed completely: fifteen regular members and nine alternates. Of the twenty-four members of the "secret directorate" of the U.S.S.R., fifteen were placed there by "K." Leadership will continue to be "collective," of course, but "K's" opinion will play about the same role as did Stalin's in his Politbureau, abolished in October, 1952, by the new party statutes which Stalin ordered Nikita Khrushchev to elaborate.

That is how "K" managed to become the *real master of the Kremlin.* But he is still not the *sole master,* as Stalin was; the situation strangely resembles the situation that existed in 1923 when Stalin, after having struck the first blows against his Trotskyite enemies, allied himself with Zinoviev and Kamenev to form his triumvirate in the Politbureau. Among the members of the present Presidium there are two who are *still capable* of preventing "K" from exercising full control. Nicolas Bulganin, the president of the council, and Georgi Zhukov, minister of war, *who has been made a member of the Presidium.*

The "economists," overwhelmed by "K's" economic reform and the creation of "sovnarkhozes," will be obliged to look for new protectors to replace Kaganovitch and Malenkov. Some of them will turn to Mikoyan, himself an "economist." But now Mikoyan is but the shadow of Nikita and most of the "economists" are more likely to lean toward Bulganin, a former Russian sovnarkhoz of the era of Lenin and Dzerzinsky and former president of the state bank. The militarists have been solidly behind Marshal Zhukov ever since his break with Zoniev at the time of his nomination of the highest military post under the Warsaw Pact.

The one really powerful force that might check Nikita is the army, *the only national instrument in the U.S.S.R.* The army has interests that coincide partially with the Molotov-Kaganovitch program (the preference for giving heavy industry first place). But the army no longer has any of the purely ideological goals which the fallen "hard-core" communists and Nikita—in spite of his program of co-existence— promoted at times. The Islamic flirtation was looked on favorably by the army, for the aim here was to create a strategic defense of the Caucasus and its petroleum and to pose a threat to the oil-rich regions of Arabia. But the liberal attitude toward the satellites and ideological co-existence with Gomulka and Tito is also to the liking of the army. Zhukov did not just happen to be actively and amicably conferring with General Gosniak, Tito's minister of war, who was then visiting in Moscow, at the exact time of the bitter struggle within the Presidium of the Russian communist party.

The Yugoslav militarists who accompanied General Gosniak reported on their arrival in Belgrade that, during a banquet given by Marshal Moskalenko, the commandant of the military region of Moscow, *there was talk of the possibility of Marshal Zhukov's occupying the post of president of the council and traveling in this capacity to the United States in the hope of reaching a definitive Russo-American agreement on disarmament with President Eisenhower.*

Perhaps Nikita Khrushchev is already thinking of transforming his triumvirate into a *duumvirate with Marshal Zhukov.*

The solidarity and power of the new triumvirate seems so strong that for the present Nikita Khrushchev has canceled, effective January 1, 1958, the forced delivery of agricultural products grown on the private plots of the peasants. Is this the first sign of a new New Economic Policy and of an era of complete liberalism in the relations between the socialist state and the non-collectivized peasantry?

If so, this might be the beginning of a Tito-type government that would pave the way for general disarmament on a world-wide scale.